TUCSON
UNCOVERED

John and Donna Kamper

Seaside Press

Library of Congress Cataloging-in-Publication Data

Kamper, John.
   Tucson uncovered / John and Donna Kamper.
      p.   cm.
   Includes index.
   ISBN 1-55622-393-5
   1. Tucson (Ariz.)—Guidebooks.   2. Tucson (Ariz.)—Description and
travel.   3. Tucson (Ariz.)—History.   I. Kamper, Donna.   II. Title.
   F819.T93K36   1995
   917.91'7760453151dc20   95-26315
                                                 CIP

ISBN 1-55622-393-5
10 9 8 7 6 5 4 3 2 1
9605

All inquiries for volume purchases of this book should be addressed to
Wordware Publishing, Inc., at 1506 Capital Avenue, Plano, Texas 75074.
Telephone inquiries may be made by calling:

(214) 423-0090

917.91

Dedication

To all the people, past, present, and future,
who have come to know and enjoy
the beauty of Tucson.

Contents

Introduction

It's the middle of August. You step outside and gaze out on a desert inhabited by rattlesnakes, jumping cactus, and tarantulas. It's so hot and the humidity so low, perspiration evaporates before it can cool you off. You have to remind yourself to drink water or you'll dehydrate before you know it.

Tucson is North America's oldest continuously inhabited settlement. The now-vanished Hohokam peoples were succeeded by other Indian tribes such as the Pima and Apache. What we now know as the Old Pueblo was first established in 1775 as Spain's northernmost outpost. Foreshadowing its diverse heritage, its founders were a Jesuit priest from Spain and a Spanish officer from Dublin.

The city lies cupped within the protective embrace of four mountain ranges. Looking down at the city's lights from these peaks after dark, the view is reminiscent of a spill of precious stones sparkling against the black velvet of the desert night.

Undeniably an Old West city, Tucson's history tells of prehistoric peoples, and Indian tribes, Spain and Mexico, Mormons, the Confederacy, and raucous times of railroads and mining, cowboys and cattle drives. While much of its appeal today lies in its mild winters, world-famous golf courses, and great Mexican food, there is much more to contemporary Tucson. Now as before, both year-round citizens and winter visitors know and love this jewel of the desert for many reasons.

Tucson continues to hold and draw on the imaginations of both residents and welcomed guests. The permanent population may now top 750,000, counting as "Tucson" the city of Tucson itself (about 500,000 population) and the Pima County area that surrounds the city and provides a suburban flair. While Tucson is a major city, it is somewhat isolated, situated in the middle of the Sonoran Desert. Phoenix lies about 120 miles to the north.

Tucson has all the amenities of large metropolitan areas like Los Angeles, Chicago, and New York, but its flavor is still that of a friendly oasis. Impatient car horns are a rarity indeed. Passersby smile and nod at each other, whether meeting downtown or on a neighborhood street. A visitor or resident can get practically anywhere in the city within a half hour, no matter what part of the city he starts from.

You'll find the residents a relaxed bunch. In the summer you won't find many businessmen with ties on. Many small businesses have minimal, if any, dress code. That may be from rubbing up against the many computer/technologically oriented businesses that are growing in number here, or because the Southwestern desert attitude has rubbed off on them. T-shirts, sleeveless shells, shorts, and sandals in the summer and jeans and cowboy boots in the winter, you'll see them all here.

We're not going to try to imply that life in Tucson is the best that it can possibly be in all areas. There's no doubt we love Tucson, but you'll see we also know it isn't perfect. We hope to uncover for you things about Tucson that are interesting while at the same time giving you an idea of what it's like to live here or visit. To that end this book includes two appendices. *For Your Information* is a list of telephone numbers of places you may find of interest. *Tucson Web Links* is for those of you who already surf the Internet (and those of you who might some day).

There's more to a place than just the people and buildings that occupy the space. This book is a look back into Tucson's history to find out what influences have shaped Tucson and its inhabitants, past and present. We also try to take a broader view, both to see how Tucson may have influenced others, and to try to estimate Tucson's viability in the modern world. From the infinite variety of the skies above to the unique flora and fauna of the Sonoran Desert, Tucson offers a wealth of treasure for all to uncover and cherish. Let's see what we can find.

CHAPTER ONE

Tucson's History

The history of a place has a remarkable influence on the people who inhabit it. This influence shows up in ways that you wouldn't recognize if you didn't have some idea of what went on in that past. Tucson is no different.

Tucson's most distinctive housing style is the territorial ranch. Adobe is one of the most visible building materials. Jalapeño peppers and Mexican food spice up its menus.

Why is Tucson such a friendly city? What are some of the influences that made Tucson what it is today? Uncovering the history and other elements that have shaped Tucson will answer some of those questions.

The most immediately noticeable influence is Tucson's climate. The City of Tucson lies in an area known in modern times as the Sonoran Desert. It's a harsh land. So harsh that in order to survive, many native plants converted their leaves to thorns. Yet this land once lay at the bottom of an inland sea.

Dinosaurs once roamed the area. A recent find southeast of Tucson is currently being studied and excavated. Then after the last ice age, much of the interior of North America was flooded. One arm of this inland sea stretched down through what is now central Arizona and reached into Mexico. You can prove this to yourself. When you go hiking in the mountains surrounding Tucson, keep your eyes open.

You may find a fossilized sea creature or shells left behind when the sea retreated.

Over the millennia, this large sea dried up. As eons progressed, mammoth, bison, and elk moved into the area, feeding in the large forests that covered the land. Men came as well, moving down in their migration from the Bering Strait and into South America. Until about 8,000 years ago, the climate in this area was quite humid. What are now desert valleys and basins were heavily wooded forests with rivers, streams, and the flora and fauna of the age.

The land and climate continued to change, becoming progressively drier. Those waterways that didn't completely dry up went, for the most part, underground. The vegetation also changed. Forests retreated and plants gradually adapted to the growing scarcity of water. As the climate became drier, the desert took hold of the land and its inhabitants.

Today's rather flat desert floor is composed of the mix of gravel, sand, and clay that has washed down from the surrounding mountain ranges. These mountains appear to rise rather abruptly out of the otherwise level land. Actually the mountains were left high and dry when the land around them sank, spread out, and formed the flat desert. Over the years, erosion has carved down the mountains and filled in the desert floor. Look at the Catalina Mountains, whose foothills compose much of northeast Tucson, and the striations in the rock are clear. The sloping angle was formed as the land fell away, not as the mountains pushed up.

The sloping angles of the mountains are due to the land falling away, not the mountains pushing up. This ridge is in the Santa Catalinas, just north of Tucson.

Early Man

The people who settled here 11,000 years ago hunted large game animals as a major food source. They used wooden spears with stone points to kill Pleistocene elephants. Points from those spears are on display in the Arizona State Museum. Hunting was done on foot, by hand, or with snares and traps.

As the climate continued to change, the larger animals became more rare. Mammoth died out, elk and bison moved more to the north. The people who remained adapted their diet to include birds, insects, and small animals. Nuts, acorns and berries, roots and bulbs, seeds and cacti fruit rounded out their diets.

This was a migratory population at first, following the game without establishing permanent locations. As the land continued to become more arid, water was found only in higher elevations with greater rainfall. Few streams ran year round on the desert floor. Those rivers, springs, and water basins which did determined where the people settled. The Sonoran Desert formed, but not the sand dune-covered, no-vegetation type of desert most people think of when the word desert comes to mind. Plants and wildlife abound here, having adapted themselves in their individual ways to the dry climate. At times the desert and mountains displayed, then as today, a lush green carpet of new growth, particularly after the rains in the spring.

Two distinct groups of people, the Hohokam and the Anasazi, are the earliest settlers identified in the Southwest. Eventually they settled throughout a large area, ranging from what is now Northern Mexico into Northern Arizona. The Anasazi lived in what is now the Phoenix area and further north. They developed a complex irrigation and agricultural economy, using water from the rivers and streams that drained the higher elevations.

The Hohokam lived in Southern Arizona and Mexico. *Hohokam* is a Pima Indian word meaning "those who have gone." These people developed both desert and riverine cultures. Those who lived near the rivers developed more stable, agrarian communities. The desert dwellers became hunter-gatherers, practicing primitive dry land agriculture without irrigation and were the first to occupy the community that is now Tucson.

These early inhabitants experienced much the same desert climate we know today. They lived here from as early as 300 B.C. until about A.D. 1000, when they seem to have vanished. Many consider the Hohokam the ancestors of the Pima Indians, who still live in the Tucson area. If you'd like an idea of how these early Tucsonans lived, visit present-day Fort Lowell Park, at 2900 North Craycroft. Evidence of a large Hohokam pit house and village has been unearthed here and is open for your exploration. It's believed this site was occupied for over a thousand years.

The Arizona State Museum at the University of Arizona also has an extensive display of this culture. (For more information about what's available at the Fort Lowell Park and Arizona State Museums among others, see Museums, page 157.)

For reasons unknown, these early inhabitants moved on, leaving a large gap in the known history of the Tucson basin. But the rivers, streams, and springs that are a part of this region remained. The river that attracted other peoples to Tucson is the Santa Cruz. These early peoples, however, wouldn't recognize it in its present stage. Now a dry river bed running north and south just to the west of downtown, it holds water only when storms or thunderstorms drop enough rain. When that happens, it turns into a raging torrent, only to dry up again soon after the sun comes out.

At one time, though, the Santa Cruz River flowed year round, guiding its life-giving water north out of Mexico. It and the smaller rivers and streams that fed into it provided a lifeline for the people who came to live near its banks. Peoples of the desert naturally came to live along the river, because in addition to providing the essential water, it also attracted game and provided trees suitable for building and land suitable for growing crops.

After the Hohokam, the people who called themselves Tohono O'odham, "people of the desert" settled this land. The Spaniards who conquered them called them Papagos, "people who eat beans," because their major crop was beans. Only recently did their descendants reclaim their true name.

These early settlements were not neatly laid out. One family or group of families settled in a general area and spread out to give each other elbow room. Others would choose an area perhaps another mile or so away. The living areas were not static but flowed through the valley, following crops as they ripened or pursuing the changing course of the river.

The name Tucson itself means "place by the black mountain." The Tohono O'odham name was "tookshon" or "schooksmon" or "stjukson." The "click" sound pronounced as the "sch-stj" consonant at the beginning of the word was lost on the Spanish, and the name became "Tucson."

The "black mountain" is probably not a specific peak but the rather small, short volcanic mountain range just west of the city. At the south end is Sentinel Peak (now called "A" Mountain, see page 156) and at the north end is Tumamoc Hill, near St. Mary's Hospital. The fresh springs there and the nearby Santa Cruz River provided a logical place to settle.

The Spanish Period

Today Tucson is as American as any other U.S. city, but when America declared its independence in 1776 Tucson was part of Mexico. Like many other Southwestern cities, the Old Pueblo's earliest European influence came from the south and Spain. The Spanish reached the New World in Mexico about a hundred years before the English arrived at Plymouth Rock. They didn't stand still, either. As were other European nations of the time, Spain was in acquisition mode. They wanted new land, riches, power, and they didn't particularly care how they got them. They were on the move.

The Spanish worked their way north into the territory that is today Arizona, Texas, New Mexico, and California long before this area of the country was influenced from the East. When an Eastern influence eventually did begin to filter in, it was an American influence, not English or European.

The Spanish influence carried its own baggage with it. Spain was a kingdom, and the king of Spain had a tightly knit organization designed not only to ensure that he receive the riches to which he claimed the right, but also to keep him in power. The Catholic Church was intimately involved in his plans. As they pushed north, the Spaniards were intent on converting the Indian peoples they met to their understanding of what it meant to be a Spanish citizen. Because the Church was an integral part of Spanish life, it was an integral part of their expansion plans. The Spanish missionaries' role was to convert the Indians to Christianity so they would be good Spanish citizens.

The military was an essential cog in the Spanish expansion machine. Not all potential Spanish citizens welcomed this conversion process, and they often put up a struggle. The defense of the Empire's progress, its converts, and its new citizens was the military's role.

When Spain began its incursions, Jesuit missionaries played the leading role for the Church. In 1694, just three years after the formation of the Massachusetts Bay Colony and still some eighty years before the Declaration of Independence, Fr. Kino, a Jesuit missionary, established San Xavier (pronounced San Ah-veer by locals) Mission near a Papago (O'odham) village, nine miles south of Tucson. The mission is still a functioning Catholic church on the Tohono O'odham Indian Reservation. (See San Xavier Mission, page 111, and Tohono O'odham, page 92.)

Tucson became a stop along the inland road to California. This "Camino Real in the making" was necessary in order to link Mexico with Southern California, where the Russians were known to be making their move at colonization.

A number of missions dotted the general area: Tumacacori, about forty miles south of Tucson on the way to Nogales; San Xavier del Bac, just south of Tucson; San Agustín del Tucson, in what is now the downtown area. This chain of missions, settlements, and military presidios experienced a number of changes over the years. Seventeen presidios stretched out over 2,000 miles from Texas to California. Soldiers were supposed to protect the peaceful

Indian settlements that formed and centered around the missions from the hostile Indians—Comanches, Navahos, some hostile Tohono O'odhams, and the feared Apaches. These presidios were intended to serve as the nuclei of new Spanish communities.

During the 1770s the settlements along the marshy Santa Cruz between Bac on the south and the Catalina Mountains to the north were too many for the soldiers to protect, so a number were consolidated. At Tucson, the Santa Cruz River, then a gentle and constantly flowing river, was the site of a large group of Tohono O'odham Indians, the logical place to consolidate. By 1771 an earthen military breastwork, or corral, equipped with gun ports, had been built at the center of the village for protection from the raiding Apaches.

At this time, Spain itself was undergoing considerable political change. The Jesuits had been forced out of their missionary role, and the Franciscan missionaries had taken their place.

In August 20, 1775, just about a year before our Declaration of Independence, a Spanish officer of Irish ancestry, one Hugo Oconor, officially recognized Tucson's existence as a Spanish presidio.

> I selected and marked out in the presence of Father Francisco Garces and Lieutenant Juan de Carmona, a place known as San Agustín del Tucson as the new site of the presidio. It is situated at a distance of eighteen leagues from Tubac, fulfills the requirements of water, pasture, and wood, and effectively closes the Apache frontier. The designation of the new presidio becomes official with the signatures of myself, Father Francisco Garces and Lieutenant Juan de Carmona, at this Mission of San Xavier del Bac, on this Twentieth day of August of the year 1775.

(Quoted from *Tucson, Portrait of a Desert Pueblo*, John Bret Harte, 1980, Windsor Publications.)

When we say Tucson has a divergent background we mean it: a Mexican/Indian village founded by an Irishman who happened to be an officer in the Spanish army.

In 1777 Captain Don Pedro de Alandre y Savedra was appointed to take command of this outpost. Luckily he was a rich man. It didn't take him too long to determine that the fortifications were insufficient for the ever-increasing Indian raids. Because Spain's purse strings were getting tighter, he had to finance the construction of a log palisade from his own funds. This palisade enclosed a guardhouse, an armory, and some other buildings that were already there.

The new fort and its relative safety attracted more Tohono O'odham Indians to it, which in turn attracted more Apache raids. The seminomadic Apaches depended on the plunder from their raids as a major part of their economy, much the same as the O'odham economy depended on agriculture and herding. The clash of the two was inevitable, and the fort proved its worth in many raids and battles. In 1782, after a particularly bloody and intense raid, the walls of the presidio were finally finished.

Three feet wide at the base, it rose to a height of ten to twelve feet. It enclosed ten acres of land and was 750 feet long on each side. The west wall paralleled *el camino real*, the "royal road" that ran all the way to Mexico City, now Main Avenue in downtown Tucson. The wall ran north along Main from what is now Pennington Street to Washington Street, and then east to Church Street. From there it turned south to what is now the old Pima County Courthouse, then west again back to Main.

This fortification is the "Old Pueblo" which gives Tucson its nickname. Like a magnet, Tucson attracted people. The closer you were to Tucson and the Old Pueblo's walls, the closer you were to protection. For centuries it was the only fortified town in the Southwest, luckily situated so that it formed the hub of the areas around it. It lasted as a fortification until the Mexican garrison left Tucson in March 1886. The U.S. Army determined that the fort was no longer appropriate as a garrison and located elsewhere. As late as the 1920s portions of the walls could still be seen, but time and expansion have left no surface evidence of "the Old Pueblo."

But to put things into perspective from the Spanish/European viewpoint: the early settlement along the Santa Cruz River some two hundred plus years ago couldn't have been the most desirable place to be stationed. It must have been considered a God-forsaken place, far from the refinements and civilization of European cities. It was, after all, the northernmost outpost of the Spanish army in the New World, in the middle of a desert, surrounded by hostile peoples. It required independence, determination, and strength of character to survive and prosper here. These characteristics remain an integral part of Tucson's personality.

In the late 1770s Tucson was a Mexican/Spanish outpost and a Mexican/Indian town, born of a much different culture than settlements in the Midwestern and Eastern parts of the country. Homes were not made of wood, neatly arranged in rows set back from the streets. There were no sidewalks or lawns to buffer homes from the noise and traffic.

Tucson was out in the middle of nowhere, and it fought to stay alive. It had little contact with the so-called civilized world that existed in the more populous areas of Mexico.

The century between 1776 and 1876 saw many changes in the growth of Tucson. The records that we have are Spanish records. Unfortunately, no record exists to tell us what the Mexicans or Indians felt was important about the presidio. In 1777 there were seventy-seven Spaniards living here (no one else counted). In 1804 the population had increased to 300, and in 1819 to 500. The total population (including Mexicans and Indians) is estimated to have been about a thousand by the year 1800.

The settlers grew corn, wheat, and vegetables. Cotton, which is now an essential agricultural crop, was grown by the Indians for their own use. There were about 3,500 head of cattle, 2,600 sheep, and about 1,200 horses. There was little local manufacturing. Soap, saddles, clothes, shoes, pots and pans, kitchen utensils, and in fact most everyday items had to be shipped in from the outside. Most of the men were engaged in agriculture or stock raising.

Until 1868, Tucson worshipers were served by the Presidio's chapel dedicated to San Agustín de Tucson. The San Xavier Mission is well to the south, about a half-day's trek by foot or horse. It wasn't until nearly a hundred years after the establishment of "El Presidio de San Agustín" that la Catedral de San Agustín was built. Its founder, Father Reghiere, began work on the Catedral in 1860 but was killed by Apaches in 1866. At that time Tucson's population was only about 600, and it took another two years for volunteers to complete the Catedral's walls.

This adobe and stone structure was located on the Plaza de la Mesilla, near what is now Broadway and Church streets. It served the Tucson faithful for only a short time, because in 1896 the new Saint Augustine Cathedral was constructed. Two years later the old building opened as a hotel. The nuns' quarters were rented out, and a dining room was installed in the nave. "Hotel St. Augustine" even featured a boxing ring on the patio.

In its last years the former church went through a number of incarnations, including a brothel in the nuns' dormitory, until it was finally converted into a garage and painted bright yellow. In 1936 the building was demolished, but its fine rose window and stone doorway, installed as the Catedral's main entrance in 1883, were saved. They now serve as the entrance to the Arizona Historical Society Museum.

Today's Saint Augustine Cathedral is located at 192 South Stone Avenue. Modeled after the Cathedral of Querétaro in Mexico, a bronze statue of Saint Augustine overlooks the entry. The facade of the building displays bas-reliefs of Arizona plants and wildlife such as the saguaro and horned toad.

The American Influence

In the late eighteenth century, events were developing in the rest of the world that would affect Tucson. Napoleon invaded Spain in the 1790s, and Spain's power was diminishing. The ruling class in Mexico was undergoing similar problems. By 1820, when the Spanish Empire was breaking up, the Tucson area felt the impact. Mexico proclaimed its independence from Spain in 1821, and the army, which was supposed to protect Tucson, weakened.

At the same time, the United States was becoming increasingly more influential. American traders, trappers, and mountain men were making their way into Northern Mexico from the east. Trade routes between Missouri settlements and New Mexico opened the way, and trade routes reached all the way to California through Tucson. So many of these traders and trappers entered the territory that the Mexican government, concerned that the number of foreigners was growing too quickly, formally protested to Washington about them.

In 1846 the two new republics of the United States and Mexico started butting heads. U.S. strategy called for sending a troop west to take Santa Fe and then continue on to California, going through disputed Arizona territory and establishing America's claim. The Mormon Battalion was sort of a caboose to the train of the "Army of the West," and it was their task to build the first road to California.

On December 17, 1846, scouts for the Mormon Battalion reached Tucson. They let their intentions of marching through the village be known, which caused considerable consternation for the commandant of the Mexican army contingent stationed there at the time. It could have been seen as an invasion by a hostile nation, and the prospect caused a lot of tension. Happily, discretion won out, and when the Battalion reached Tucson the Mexican army had conveniently decamped south to San Xavier Mission. The confrontation was avoided, and the event passed without trouble.

The Mormon Battalion was responsible for completing the wagon road to California, a major undertaking. They finally reached California in January 1847. Their road became the east-west corridor for thousands of homesteaders and miners now making their way west. Mesa, now a Phoenix suburb, contains a major Mormon population whose origins date back to those times.

More and more Americans were finding their way to Tucson. When gold was discovered in California in 1849 the way west for many miners led through Tucson. Americans were no longer a novelty in town, and trade with the Americans was growing.

By the late 1850s Tucson was still a Mexican village, but by now it provided its own means for daily living. There were no roads as such, but Tucson was the most important town in the region. Because it was also fortified, it was often "the Good Ol' Pueblo." People found their way there naturally, following the paths laid out by similar travelers throughout the years. Eventually stagecoaches and wagons found their way there.

Business interests wanted a southern railroad route to the West Coast. On June 29, 1854, as part of the Gadsden Treaty, one of a number of favorable treaties the United States entered into with Mexico after the Mexican/American War, Congress bought about 30,000 square miles of new territory, which included Tucson, for $10 million, a transaction known as the Gadsden Purchase.

Tucson "suddenly" became American. It had become a part of the New Mexico Territory. But things didn't change overnight. This was still the very Wild West, and the local residents still needed protection from the Indian raids that took place with frequency. The Mexican army stayed to offer protection from the raiding Apaches until American troops arrived in 1856.

Business was good in Tucson in 1860. The population was increasing, but with the increase came all the usual problems that accompany prosperity. Newcomers to town were of all kinds, from settlers with a high moral character to desperate men who lived by the gun, their wits, or a combination of both. Gambling halls, prostitutes, and drinking establishments were abundant. Tucson could have been the model for any of those Wild West towns depicted in the movies. (It later was. See Old Tucson, page 109.) Samuel W. Cozzens, who visited Tucson in 1859, wrote, "Probably never before in the history of any country were gathered within the walls of a city such a complete assortment of horse-thieves, gamblers, murderers, vagrants, and villains."

There weren't many "snowbirds" back then, and tourist accommodations could most kindly be described as haphazard. Any visitor, however, was welcome to a "Tucson bed," where you lie down on your stomach and "cover yourself with your back." There were other alternatives for travelers, of course; you could always lie down on your back, and pull your front up over you.

Like most Western towns at the time, there were a significant number of lawless men. There were also a significant number of local citizens who wanted more and better from the town where they'd settled. In time, families were raised, schools were started, trade was encouraged, and transportation routes were established.

As before, there was a need for protection, both military (because the Indians were still a problem) and legal (because of the general lawlessness in the area). Tucson did not have a working judicial district, and there was no organized law. Arizona was not yet officially recognized as a separate American territory. There was a significant amount of home-grown political pressure to bring it into the Nation, but the Civil War interrupted the process.

Tucson was split in allegiance between the North and the South. Many Western towns were, but more definitely leaned towards the South. Confederate sympathizers outnumbered Unionists in Tucson. What the people of the New Mexico Territory, including Tucson, *really* wanted was protection from the Indians (does the name Geronimo ring a bell?) and the Mexican bandits who raided from across the border. The town petitioned the Confederate Congress for an army.

The Confederates eventually sent troops, but any concern for the safety of the citizens of Tucson was secondary. Tucson was a critical way station on the road to California and other western areas that could provide needed gold, silver, food, and sympathizers to the Confederate cause. Tucson was strategically located.

The Union recognized the geographical importance of Tucson as well, and it wasn't far behind. Its California Brigade was advancing from California. There was a brief encounter of the two armies near Yuma, and the Confederates retreated. A larger and more important skirmish occurred near Picacho Peak, about forty miles north of Tucson. It was just that, a skirmish. A few men were killed, but it was so obvious that the Union army outnumbered the Confederates that the Confederates withdrew.

The Union troops continued on to Tucson and occupied the town. The main body of Confederate soldiers had left earlier, so there was no conflict. Occupation by the Union troops brought some peace to the town, although some may have denied it. In fact, many citizens thought that the soldiers created more problems in the growing city than the Indians did.

It wasn't until February 20, 1886, that the Territory of Arizona became a legal entity. Tucson would have been the site of the Territory Headquarters, but the lingering Confederate influence was too strong for the conquering Union, and a different site, Prescott, was chosen.

After the Civil War a good degree of lawlessness returned to the city. For many people it was a disheartening place. The presence of Camp Lowell and Union troops in town made life difficult for many. Off-duty soldiers drank too much, shot off their firearms in town, and in general were considered a nuisance. Besides that, they weren't doing much to ward off raiding Apaches. In 1872 the soldiers were moved to a new post, built on the northeast of town and renamed Fort Lowell. Today you can still see the crumbling remains of its adobe walls at Fort Lowell Park (see page 161).

Tucson was no better or worse than most other Wild West towns. In 1870 Tucson was incorporated as a village with a mayor and councilmen, but the newspapers of the day were filled with reports of killings, shootings, lynchings, all manner of lawlessness, and western justice. Gunslingers and desperadoes were still common. The first marshal in Tucson was William Morgan, who served for only three months. John Miller, an even tougher lawman, took his place. There's the popular story about the outlaw Bill Brazelton who held up the same stagecoach.

In 1878 the stage was on its regular run from Tucson to Florence. In the late afternoon heat the horses were walking up a sandy section of the trail when an outlaw stepped out from behind some bushes. He aimed a rifle at the driver and stopped the stage. The armed bandit wore a white sack with eye-holes cut out of it and a red bandanna sewn into place as a mouth. He threatened to shoot anyone who tried to stop him, promising them that he could shoot one or two of them before they could kill him. With six-gun in hand he robbed the passengers and the stage and sent it on its way again. His earnings? About forty dollars and a pair of earrings.

The next week the same driver was on the same stage, driving the same route, but this time one of his passengers was Sheriff John Miller. As the driver, Arthur Hill, was coming to the same sandy trail, he pointed the bush out to the sheriff where the robber had appeared before. To his and Miller's surprise the outlaw was standing there again in the same get-up. There was an express box and some mail on the stage, so the robber got about $250. Sheriff Miller got a good look at the horse and a good description of the man. Later that night, Pima County Sheriff Charlie Shibell and a tracker followed the outlaw's trail headed south.

They eventually found the horse at the ranch of David Nemitz, who denied knowing anything about the holdups. He was arrested anyway and held in jail. Two days later he admitted that the holdup man was Bill Brazelton and that he was afraid Bill would kill him if he told.

Brazelton was a Tucson citizen. He had been employed at a stable in downtown Tucson and was rather well liked. It was discovered that Brazelton had been responsible for a number of robberies. A posse was soon rounded up and a trap set. They had Nemitz arrange a meeting with Brazelton and waited in the dark for him. When Nemitz gave the sign that Brazelton was the man approaching, the posse gunned him down without warning. They didn't take chances in those days.

No one ever found out what Brazelton did with the money he stole. Some stories estimate his total take at over $10,000. There are stories that he buried it somewhere, making a hit with modern-day treasure hunters.

Since the Gadsden Purchase, ownership of land had been slowly passing to Anglos. Most of its 3,000 plus citizens were engaged in some sort of business, and Tucson was growing in importance as a center of trade and transportation.

As American technology spread west, Tucson became more Americanized. The majority of the citizens wanted a decent place to live. A telephone exchange was installed in 1881, gaslights in 1882, water pipes were laid to supply fresh water to homes, and fire departments were organized by 1883. Even then, Tucson was at the forefront of change.

Although civilization was encroaching, Apaches were still on the warpath. Indian leaders such as Geronimo, Chato, and Cochise were among those causing trouble.

By 1881 there was an established police force consisting of six men. It took time, but the frontier town was being tamed.

In 1885 the Arizona Territorial Government was allocating institutions. Tucson was in the running to become the state capital. Other prizes to be bargained for were the state insane asylum and a state university.

Much to its chagrin at the time, Tucson was awarded the university instead of the capital designation. It could have been worse. Tucson is much happier with the world-renowned University of Arizona making its home here than it would be with the insane asylum, which was established in Phoenix.

A saloon keeper and two gamblers donated forty acres of their land to house the university. After a number of years in formation the University of Arizona was finally opened. At first its courses were geared to the mining industry. As agriculture became more important, the school added agronomy classes. The first class of three students was graduated in 1885.

Mining was becoming more important in Arizona. One of the largest mines in the area was in Tombstone. A fellow by the name of Al Schieffeline was persistent in his search for gold. When everyone else was hiding from the Indians and trying to stay alive, he was out digging. Soldiers used to tell him that he would find nothing there but his tombstone. When he took some of the ore he found into Tucson to assay it, they tried to talk him into farming.

He and two partners stuck with it and struck it rich, with ore that assayed at $9,000 of silver to the ton. The company paid out $50,000 a month in dividends. This of course brought other miners to the area with the result that Schieffeline named the place Tombstone. It was this silver discovery in Tombstone that eventually brought the railroad to Tucson. The price of silver declined in the late 1880s because silver was no longer used on coins, and mining it soon declined as an industry.

Freighting was an important industry during and after the Civil War. When the Butterfield Overland Mail closed down, there was little transportation across the Territory. The largest hauling firm was Tully and Ochoa. Wagons and teams the company owned were estimated to have the value of over $100,000. There were hundreds of men who hauled goods for the firm, loaded and unloaded the wagons, and took care of the horses. They had the handle on supplying the goods for all the government posts and Indian reservations in the area.

When the railroad came to town there was a lot of celebrating, but not by the freight companies. They couldn't compete with the cheap rates of the railroads, and most went out of business.

Modern Tucson

By the end of the nineteenth century, technology was making Tucson a modern city. After the railroads came, automobiles, airplanes, roads, and their accompanying industries made their way here.

Mining, which had lured men to the area for decades, burgeoned again and came into its own. Copper mines surround Tucson. Some of their tailings, large and plateau-like, are visible in the desert southwest of Tucson. During the Second World War, copper was one of Arizona's "Three C's": Copper, Climate, and Cotton.

Agriculture found a way to irrigate the desert fields, and cotton became the favorite cash crop. Many people from colder areas of the country found that the thin desert air aided their pneumonia, and Tucson became a haven for sanitoriums. Davis Monthan Air Force Base brought men and women to Tucson from every area of the United States. Companies recognized Tucson as a good base for their businesses or for regional offices. The combination saw Tucson's population greatly increase.

The many changes in technology, communication, and life-style of the United States after WWII saw Tucson, now an established United States city, grow up with the rest of the world.

Tucson has also carved its niche in the modern business world. NAFTA, our recent trade agreement with Mexico and Canada, has opened a modern doorway into Mexico. Tucson is a distribution center for many businesses. Several high-tech industries, such as Hughes, Burr-Brown, and others have located here. Microsoft, the personal computer software industry's leader, is the newest addition. Tucson is known as the "optic valley" for the optic industry, and the University of Arizona continues to excel in its many fields of study.

As with most cities of the world, Tucson is a composite of many different influences. Mixed up in its "genes" are the influences of Mexico, Spain, Indians and cowboys, miners, trappers and traders, villains and heros. Today the city's personality is recognized for its openness, frankness, friendliness, and independence.

You may have to be somewhat of an individualist to enjoy living here (Tucson is in the middle of a desert, after all), but visitors find that everyone is welcome. Many have discovered the same elements that originally attracted the earliest peoples to the "black mountain" and fostered our growth and development are still very much in effect. The Old Pueblo still provides a place in the desert to be glad you're in. Welcome to Tucson!

CHAPTER TWO

Jewel of the Desert

When you learn that Tucson is the oldest continuously inhabited site in the Americas, you may wonder what has attracted so many people to it throughout the ages. Tucsonans —of all times—consider the city the Jewel of the Desert.

The setting of a special stone is often just as important as the gem itself. This holds true for Tucson as well. It lies in an open desert valley surrounded by the protective arms of four different mountain ranges. This is the setting for the jewel of the desert.

Tucson is a vibrant city, full of active people. Its setting—from the desert floor to the highest peak—fosters this activity.

The Sky Above

One of the first things people notice about Tucson is the sky—it's hard to miss. Tucson's architecture tends to be low, so even in the heart of downtown there's an open, expansive feeling with horizons far in the distance, connected by the extraordinary blue dome of sky arching far overhead.

The second thing people notice are the mountains, part of the city. The Tucson Mountains on the west are easy to spot with "A" Mountain out in front and flanked by more distant mountains further back. The Catalinas are the mountains rising abruptly to the north, cutting short Tucson's immediate northern horizon. To the east are the Rincon Mountains, setting the stage for sunrise. To Tucson's south are the Santa Rita Mountains, far enough away that from the city they appear small on the horizon. The wide valley floor, formed in large part by alluvium from these four mountain ranges, provides a magnificent viewing platform for the vast sky overhead.

The Tucson Mountains are on the west side of the city. You can see them from many places in the city. Here they form a backdrop to the University of Arizona campus.

The Santa Catalina Mountains as they appear from a distance to the south. The mountains fall suddenly from a series of large canyons and ridges and immediately spill into their foothills. (Photo courtesy of Kevilee Schaich)

The Santa Rita Mountains lie far to the south. Their distant outline forms our southern horizon.

23

Drive north on Campbell, Swan, or Craycroft roads into the Catalina foothills which are still within the city limits. As you gain elevation you can see behind you just how wide and far the valley is. At night the lights of the city are spread out before you, a "necklace of a million lights."

Depending on the season, the ever-changing skies provide different backgrounds for desert views. In summer skies are an intense, brilliant blue. The high pressures that settle over the area tend to bring clear, hot weather, and they intensify in the summer. When one of these "domes" settles over the Southwestern U.S., the sky empties of clouds and the sun is brilliant. The higher the barometric pressure, the more particulates, dust, and other elements are forced out of this high pressure zone. Because the air is unobscured, the sky becomes a deep, royal blue. When you look straight up, it's as if you can see forever!

> ❏ In addition to the sky being big, it's also brilliant and bright. Don't forget your sunglasses! The sun can be quite glaring during the middle of the summer. A good pair of sunglasses, especially ones that screen out UV rays, isn't a smart accessory in Tucson. It's just smart.

Because of the expansive horizons, often a variety of type, shape, color, and texture of clouds fill the skies. The northeast edge of the horizon may display the wispy streamers of mares' tails (cirrus clouds), while thunderheads (cumulonimbus) are marching up from the south, towering up to eight miles high in the atmosphere.

Tucson's clouds have a starring role at sunset. Living in a desert has some definite perks, and the sunsets are in the top two. The light of the setting sun, filtered through atmospheric dust in the far distance, dyes the clouds completely across the sky from west to east.

Photography buffs enjoy the challenge of capturing this incredible natural display, but it's difficult to imagine any

Thunderheads building up over Tucson

photograph doing justice. The best way to take one of Tucson's sunsets back with you is inside your head.

To capture a sunset you can replay at leisure, pick a day with a fair number of clouds in the west. Plan your trip so you get there about a half-hour or so before actual sunset. Drive west on Speedway Boulevard until you get to Gate's Pass, about ten minutes west of the I-10 freeway in Tucson Mountain Park. That's where you can really take advantage of the view. Once you are over the Pass there are a number of turnoffs. There are some picnic ramadas in the park there, with an ample parking lot. Don't pull into a camping area unless you're sure the rangers won't be locking it up, or you could wind up staying there all night. If you pull off alongside the road, make sure you're off far enough not to be a hazard to anyone, yourself included.

Take along something cold to drink, some folding chairs, and settle down facing west. Here you have a wide panorama for sunset watching. You may see what looks like waves of pink cotton candy. This is virga, over-eager rain that falls prematurely from water-laden clouds but evaporates long before reaching the ground. Then the pink deepens to a deep red color, until sometimes the sky itself seems to be on fire. Beams of sunlight spill through the clouds, golden rays reaching to all directions.

You don't have to go to Gates Pass to enjoy the sunset. When clouds and conditions are right, sunsets cover the sky from horizon to horizon. Enjoy them from your backyard or just walking down the street.

Even after the sun is completely under the horizon, the show continues for a long time. The colors deepen, then fade, and then the stars come out.

The Sun on the Mountains

Of course, it's not just the clouds that get washed with colors. The mountains themselves are just as great a show.

When the sun rises over the Rincon Mountains, the first to catch its rays are the Catalinas. Watching this range at dawn, you see that the gradually increasing light slowly picks out the separate elements of the mountains. As the light warms in intensity, Pusch Ridge begins to gleam and Thimble Peak seems to move forward.

Then the first glint of sunlight peeks over the Rincons, and a rosy blush suddenly washes the top of the entire south face of the Catalinas. The blush deepens a bit, then fades as the sun grows higher. Shadows move and dance through the peaks and valleys until the entire mountain seems to be alive.

As the sun rises higher, it blanches out the shadows, and the mountains take on a flat appearance. The overhead sun washes out the demarcations of the various loops and curves of the ranges and canyons.

Usually air is invisible, especially Tucson's clear, clean desert air. But there are some days, usually in the afternoon but well before sunset, when the air turns heavy and the lowering sun paints the mountains a golden hue. You've heard of rose-colored glasses? When this happens you're looking through lenses with a golden tint, and the mountains are bathed in an intense glow.

Sunrise may paint a rosy pink, and some afternoons can bring a golden haze, but sunsets—sunsets are a bit more gaudy. (Just a bit.) Watching the sunset from Gate's Pass allows you to concentrate just on the sunset and its effects on the clouds. Watch a sunset from anywhere within the Tucson valley and you enjoy an additional attraction, the special lighting effects on the mountains.

The changing angle of the sunlight creates stark contrasts in the appearance of the surrounding mountains. Features that had never before been apparent suddenly leap out at the viewer. Shadows cast by high ridges seem to create deep canyons. Rock faces that appeared blinding white at noon suddenly reflect purples, violets, and pink hues.

When the sun slips below the horizon, much of the definition of the mountain disappears. Slowly the different protrusions and recessions blend together in the deepening gloom of the twilight. Even after all light has drained from the sky, even on moonless nights, the mountains' edge is often visible against the darkening night sky. And then the stars come out. . . .

Clouds stoop lower in the winter. Tucson is about 2,400 feet above sea level (2,389 to be exact), so they don't have to stoop much. When clouds do dip down across the mountain ranges, an entire new dimension enters the picture. The Catalina Mountains are so close and up-front to the north of the city that the two merge together. You can easily forget the collection of peaks and canyons contained in them. The three-dimensional actuality of these mountains may not be fully appreciated until you notice the clouds playing "can't catch me!" through their canyons.

As the clouds roll across the mountains at different elevations, suddenly the mountains as a whole seem to pull back and away from your view. Separate and distinct features appear from what seemed a flat background moments ago. A three-dimensional mountain range suddenly thrusts itself forward from a two-dimensional backdrop.

The clouds turn the mountain range into a fan-dancer, alternatively hiding and pulling aside, teasing us with glimpses and hints of beauty yet unveiled. Thimble Peak, the sentinel of Sabino and Bear Canyons to the northeast of the city, at times is the sole representative of the entire Catalina range. A cuff of clouds cuts Finger Rock, on the west end of the range, loose from the mountain below, leaving it pointing heavenward as the mountain's sole representative.

Occasionally a long streamer of cloud snags around one of the larger peaks, for all the world a fleecy stole draped

Thimble Peak stands guard over Sabino Canyon, on the northeast side of Tucson.

Finger Rock, flanked by two other peaks, points its bony digit to the sky above. (Photo courtesy of Kevilee Schaich)

around a rocky goddess's shoulders. Snippets of clouds crouch across the top of a ridge like cats ready to spring, or one peeks over the ridge for all the world like Kilroy.

During winters the desert mountains sometimes turn white, surprising visitors. Yes, sometimes Tucson does have snow! Winter clouds bring snow annually to the tops of the Catalinas, and sometimes the Rincon range is capped during a cold snap. It's an interesting sight on a cold morning. Because the desert floor is too warm for snow except on rare occasions, the snow only comes so far down the slopes, ending abruptly as if a ruler's edge was used. When conditions are just right, even the city itself gets a white dusting.

Mount Lemmon is the highest peak in the Catalina Mountains, at 9,157 feet. Mt. Lemmon Ski Valley welcomes visitors and residents alike to its ski lodge from late December through April (snow permitting). Snow in the valley never lasts long, but skiing at Mt. Lemmon is a mere thirty-five-mile drive up from the desert floor. Also on Mt. Lemmon,

Summerhaven (as its name implies) offers a respite from the desert's heat.

Monsoons in the Desert

Another season in Tucson that brings spectacular skies is midsummer, when the monsoons arrive. This is the season of the thunderbird. At this time of the year the humidity increases markedly. Heat boils up from the desert. Thunderstorms form when the two combine. This increase in humidity, accompanied by high pressure and escalating temperatures, causes giant columns of thunderclouds to build over the intense blue desert skies. Depending on conditions, the clouds may spend most of the afternoon building in power against their blue background.

As the sun drifts to the west it turns these thunderheads so brightly sun-white at their tops, you can barely look at them. Down below, their characteristic flat anvil-like bases are dark and rumbling, lightning flashes already punctuating the skies.

Many times you "smell" the rain long before it comes down. The increase in humidity tends to muffle sounds. There's a heaviness and moistness to the air. Then when the rainstorm has passed there's a freshness, a "scrubbed" element that enters the air. The hot, rain-soaked ground steams, bringing a heavy scent that evokes thoughts of green growth.

Depending on the temperature difference between the ground and the clouds, before the rain (or instead of rain) you may see virga. These are gray sheets of falling rain that evaporate long before they reach the ground. The moisture and energy is pumped back up into the clouds, building up power for later releases. The humidity continues to increase, and then suddenly the skies seem to open. Sometimes the rain comes down so hard you can't see across the street. Arizonans ('Zonies) call that kind of storm a frog-strangler, or gully-washer. No matter how hard or gentle the downpour, however, half an hour after the storm has passed the ground is dry.

> ❏ You will learn, however, that there are certain streets in Tucson it's wise to avoid during (and immediately after) rain. (Drainage system? This is a desert! In large part, the streets *are* the drainage system in the desert.)

If you are caught driving in a downpour, one word of advice. Believe the barricades. If water is flowing across the street and a traffic cone or a sawhorse bars your way, don't go around it and try to ford across. If you see someone already stuck, don't think you can make it when they didn't.

In 1994 the Arizona legislature passed the so-called "stupid-motorist law." Under its provisions, drivers who ignore barricades and get trapped in flooded areas are liable for up to $2,000 in rescue expenses, plus a $500 fine.

The Tucson area has many washes that are dry and unnoticeable most of the time. They quickly fill with water after storms, even if the storms are out in the desert or in the mountains, miles away from a specific location.

This water, whether flowing through desert gullies, washes, or streets, runs fast and furious and is not to be trifled with. Many streets, particularly on the outskirts, follow the original contours of the land. That means roads have been built crossing natural waterways. Even downtown! That yardstick painted on the Stone Avenue underpass isn't just for decoration. When the clouds break loose, the water continues to follow courses created millennia ago. If you (or your car) happen to be in the way, you'll be treated just like any other piece of debris and carried downstream.

If the clouds overhead are thunderheads, lightning is a definite possibility. Tucson is known for its beautiful lightning displays, both in the valley and over the surrounding mountains.

Lightning can also be dangerous. Anytime you're outdoors in the desert—hiking, biking, or playing golf—pay attention to the weather. If a storm is coming, you'll be able to tell—the clouds, the humidity (the big booms). Sudden thunderstorms are common in the desert and frequently bring lightning (thunder = lightning). Whether you hear big booms or not, if your hair starts to stand on end, you have a serious electrical situation approaching. This is not good! If you're out golfing, take the prescribed remedy to avoid being struck by lightning: get off the course. You're safest indoors during an electrical storm.

If you're outside when rain threatens, follow common-sense precautions. Stay away from objects that attract lightning: trees and power poles, bodies of water, and metallic objects like wire fences. Don't be the tallest object around, either. Stay low, and don't shelter under anything likely to attract lightning. (Palm trees are a very popular target for lightning, by the way.) If you're in an automobile, stay in it. Otherwise, seek safe cover from the rain.

If you're out in open desert and a thunderstorm catches you and lightning is striking nearby, the prescribed position is to crouch down into a little ball. Don't stretch out flat. Make yourself as small as possible. If you find yourself on your knees in this position, a prayer or two wouldn't hurt.

Diamonds on Black Velvet

Desert skies have long been a mecca for stargazers. The clarity of desert air and the distance from large light sources have drawn astronomers to Tucson for years. Mention astronomy and Tucson in the same sentence, and people think of Kitt Peak, perhaps Tucson's most famous observatory. There are many other observatories in the Tucson area, among them Flandrau Planetarium at the University of Arizona.

If you drive out of town in practically any direction for fifteen minutes, you can easily find a place dark enough to get away from the glare. Even within Sabino Canyon, barely on the outskirts of town, the canyon walls shield most of the light from the city so that the skies are dark black. The

Milky Way floats over the sky, and the constellations march across the night. You could make it a tradition to watch the annual Perseid meteor showers in August from the parking lot there.

Daylight Savings Time

One of the best ideas Ben Franklin ever came up with, in the eyes of some, was Daylight Savings. Under this plan everyone sets their clocks ahead one hour in the spring, and then in the fall they turn them back. It was during World War I that this system first came into use in Europe, but not until World War II did the U.S. adopt it, in both cases for purposes of energy conservation.

After the war ended, there was a lot of haggling back and forth over the subject in this country until 1966, when Congress established the Uniform Time Act. Under that law every state was obliged to adopt Daylight Saving time unless the state's legislature specifically voted not to.

Surprise—Arizona's legislature decided to be contrary. The net result is that Arizona does not change times with the rest of the United States. From April through October, it has the same time as Pacific Daylight time. From November through March it follows Mountain Standard time.

The sky above holds many wonderful sights and beauties in Tucson. Our sky is wide and our horizons far. But no matter how far out they stretch, we live in the land below.

The Land Below

It's a Dry Heat

Tucsonans joke a lot about dry heat. In truth, the searing summer heat lasts for only a couple of months out of the year. If it weren't for low humidity, the heat would be

unbearable. But Tucson's low humidity and high temperatures do require some special attention. For instance, true
'Zonies:

- Automatically throw a towel over the steering wheel
  whenever they park the car.
- Don't care how far away they have to park, as long
  as it's in the shade.
- Know better than to sit down on plastic seat covers.
- Or for that matter, any other medium that sits in the
  sun. Arizona children learn early on that slides in
  the sun are not their friends.
- Wear shoes with an R-factor high enough to protect
  feet from the melting asphalt or tar.
- Wear light-colored, loose-fitting clothes (a bed sheet
  works just fine).

And even today,

- Don't care which movie is playing or if the menu
  features burgers or escargot. The only question
  asked is "Are you air-conditioned?"

In deep summer, a daytime high temperature of about
110 degrees isn't uncommon, but that's with a humidity
factor of 10 percent or less. Those who were in the Midwest
and East in the summer of 1995 when temperatures reached
100 degrees plus may wonder how Tucsonans put up with
their temperatures. Well, when you factor in the humidity
the temperatures during that Midwest heat wave were really more in the 120-130 degree range. With the desert's
general lack of humidity Tucson doesn't see that kind of
heat. Too, in Tucson they're geared up for temperatures
over 100 degrees. People dress for it, homes are designed for
it, and besides, it *is* a dry heat.

> ❏ Low or high humidity, a parked car with its windows up, even one in the shade, can reach 200 degrees in as little as 15 minutes, depending on the outside temperature. **Don't** leave people or pets in the car while you "run inside for just a minute." You could return to tragedy.

While it's low humidity that makes 110 degrees "bearable," this causes its own problems. You may not perspire (oh heck, this is Tucson; let's say sweat) noticeably except underneath a backpack/fannypack. Sweat that appears on exposed skin evaporates almost immediately, keeping you relatively cool. The downside is that you don't notice you're losing water, and you can dehydrate quickly. If there's a little breeze, or if you're moving, the sweat evaporates even more quickly. Getting dried out in the desert can happen quickly.

The saying is, "If you're thirsty, you're already dehydrated." In the summer, many Tucsonans carry a squeeze-bottle of water with them almost everywhere—in the car, to the shopping mall, the grocery store, even the office. The ubiquitous water bottle takes many shapes, from the simple type that fits onto bicycles to insulated designer models.

Low humidity may also make your skin drier. The sun bakes most things in the desert, your skin included. Many women (and men) find their skin is drier here than it's ever been before.

> ❏ To keep the "itchies" away use a rich moisturizing soap, and consider bath oil. Buy a small spray bottle and fill it with your favorite bath oil. While still wet after your bath or shower, spray yourself all over before toweling off.

When outdoors, use sun block. Choose a high number, and apply liberally. Not only will it protect you from the sun's ultraviolet light rays (which are pretty intense here), it will also help moisturize your skin. If you have children, make sure they use it. A bad sunburn ruins the day, no matter who gets it.

Many people stay inside when it gets very hot. Others think that is just the time to get out and experience the desert. Fine, but take precautions. Wear a hat. If you're out in the desert, make sure you carry water with you, and take a good drink every fifteen minutes or so. The experts advise one gallon per person per day as a minimum, but you should realize that an exercising adult in the sun can sweat as much as two quarts an hour.

If you are out in the sun and heat, you should know some of the symptoms of overexposure. There are three different types of heat-related illness: heat cramps, heat exhaustion, and heat stroke.

A heat cramp is the mildest form and is basically a muscle cramp. Someone playing tennis in the heat, for example, may get a leg cramp. Rest and drinking fluids is the usual remedy.

Symptoms of heat exhaustion are dizziness, weakness, nausea, thirst, and vomiting. Healthy adults with these symptoms should get out of the heat immediately, sip cool fluids, and fan themselves. An elderly person with heat exhaustion, or someone who doesn't respond quickly, should see a doctor.

Heat stroke is a life-threatening emergency. The body's temperature rises and the person appears to be very confused, on the verge of passing out, or has lost consciousness. Call an ambulance. Move the victim out of the heat and cool the person off. Put wet cloths or cold packs around the neck and in the armpits and groin areas.

If you plan to spend some time driving around the area, go prepared. No matter where you live, it's a good idea to travel with some essentials in a small box in your trunk.

Start with water. Particularly if you intend to drive out of the city limits, make sure you bring water with you. In addition to the cold water you bring with you inside the car, put a gallon of water in that box in the trunk. While you're at it, throw in another gallon for the radiator. There's no doubt about it, water is the most important element in the desert. If you happen to get stuck somewhere, even that hot water in the trunk will be welcome. Actually, a gallon for each seatbelt is ideal.

> ❑ A gallon a day is the minimum per person per day in the desert. In 1995 two people drove off the road to catch a nap and look at the desert. They were only going from "here to there," not camping out or hiking. They had no supplies, no water. They had car trouble eight miles off the road. Within three days one died and the other barely made it. The desert is unforgiving.

The desert cools down surprisingly fast after sunset, and again the low humidity is responsible. Whether up on one of the mountains or on the desert floor, nights can get pretty chilly. Throw a lightweight thermal blanket into the box— one of those foil-like "space blankets" is ideal. Add sunscreen, granola bars, paper towels (even better, some pre-moistened wipes), a pocket comb and tweezers (for removing cactus thorns), a flashlight with an extra pack of new batteries, a mirror for signaling, and maybe a first-aid kit. Tuck the box into your trunk, and you've got a well-stocked desert emergency kit.

You might think this is a waste of time. After all, you'll be using paved roads and highways, not driving roughshod through the desert, won't you? Probably so. But in general it's a long ways from any one place to another in Arizona. Even if you have a cellular phone, it still takes time for roadside assistance to reach you. And if the stop is unplanned, chances are you won't have brought along a picnic lunch.

Another rule for the desert: Don't strip down for the sun. It's much better to wear loose, light-colored clothing than go bare-shouldered or hatless. The desert sun is fierce and burns much faster than the sun in northern climates. Tanning isn't something you have to work on in Tucson. Use sunscreen liberally and often. Especially on children! We tend to forget they're out in the sun much more than we sedentary adults. Sunglasses that screen out UV rays are a wise accessory and are recommended for children as well as adults.

The summer heat affects the area's building styles as well. The first inhabitants of this land built low to the ground. In the ground, in fact, at least in part. The Hohokam people lived in houses with floors about a foot below ground level. They made their walls of thick adobe bricks to keep the heat out in the summer and the cold out in the winter. This practice has been a feature of the desert ever since. Thick walls, like the adobe walls of the old haciendas, are a common feature of Southwestern architecture.

Another feature adapted to Tucson's low humidity is the cooler. For years the only way to cool down in the summer was to use an evaporative cooler, what 'Zonies call a swamp cooler. These metal cubes perch atop many Tucson homes.

As water evaporates it cools. A swamp cooler works on that principle. Inside the cooler is a large pad of straw (or some more modern material) that is kept saturated with water by rotating through a pan filled with water. A large fan blows air through the wet pad, down through ducts, and into the house. Because normal desert humidity is between 8 percent and 20 percent, the water quickly evaporates and reduces the temperature, some say by as much as twenty degrees when it's the hottest. Until the monsoons come, that is.

During the monsoon season in mid-July and August, when the humidity increases drastically (as high as what some other states consider normal), swamp coolers don't work because the moisture doesn't evaporate. That's when the air conditioner comes into its own. Many Tucsonans use a swamp cooler during the hot, dry weather (saving their utility budget), and leave the air conditioner unused except for that brief period when the humidity mounts.

Cacti and Desert Flowers

Much of Tucson's desert fauna seems unfriendly to a visitor's eyes. Ages ago when the inland sea receded and the land became a desert, the plants that survived were the ones that adapted to the changing climate. Leaves became thorns, stems became water reservoirs, and roots learned to travel great distances for water. Many of the desert plants belong to the cactus family.

Cacti didn't drop all their leaves when they adapted to the desert. Some became poreless spines, thus cutting down on water loss. Not only protection against browsers, cactus thorns also channel moisture to the plant's roots. The shadows cast by the spines, as thin as they are, also provide valuable shade during the day.

Up to 90 percent of a cactus may be water. Extraordinarily shallow-rooted when their overall size is considered, very few cacti have taproots. The saguaro is one that does, but it only goes two to three feet deep. Even cacti with taproots spread a shallow net of roots wide around the plant, to "drink" as much as possible during a rainstorm. During dry weather, the stored water is parceled out to sustain the plant.

The ribbed construction shared by almost all erect cacti allows the plant to take in enormous amounts of water, stretching out the skin between them and, in very wet years, rounding outward. During dry times the plant shrinks between the ribs without damage as the stored water is used up.

Cacti played an elementary part in the everyday life of Native Americans. Saguaro ribs were used for building. The saguaro's edible fruit played an important element of the Tohono O'odham's diet and in their New Year celebrations. The prickly pear and cholla also have edible fruit. Prickly pear pads are used in meals today. The agave provided cord, twine, and string from its fiber, and needles from its spines.

It's also the base for tequila and mescal. Ocotillo wands make a fearsome fence, all the more so when the wands root themselves and begin to grow.

Thorn Alert

Where there is cactus, there are thorns. There are three varieties of cactus thorns, big, medium, and invisible but deadly. The first two are fairly easy to spot, but it's the last variety that really makes an impression.

Cactus spines are commonly hollow and barbed at the end (some varieties more so than others). If the spines break, the barbs may remain embedded in the skin. If you're stuck, make sure you get all the spines out and then wash the area thoroughly to avoid infection.

The cholla and prickly pear varieties of cactus surround the base of their large visible spines with a fringe of tiny,

Prickly pear cactus with fruit. The dots at the base of the thorns and covering the fruit at the edges of the pads are the extremely small, thin, and sharp glochid thorns common to both the prickly pear and cholla cactus.

hairlike thorns. These are called glochids. If you look at a prickly pear fruit, you'll see a sort of polka-dot pattern scattered over it. The polka-dots are clumps of glochids. These are almost impossible to see once you've got them in your skin, but you can sure feel 'em. Here's where tweezers come in handy, and maybe even a magnifying glass.

When large chunks of cactus attach themselves to you (usually this is a cholla segment), a pocket comb is recommended. Hold the comb close to the skin and slide the teeth of the comb through the spines. Then carefully pull the cactus away from the skin. If you try to just pick one off, it rolls merrily along, sticking and pricking its way as it goes.

Saguaro

Probably the most-recognized cactus around Tucson is the saguaro (sah-whár-oh). You can see them anywhere in the Tucson area. As you drive down the freeway, they are the tall sentinels that appear to be marching along the road with arms held high.

The saguaro is found only in the Sonoran Desert, growing only on this one place on earth. A mature saguaro may weigh twelve tons, most of which is water. Some are fifty to sixty feet tall and may have a life span up to 200 years. A famous giant saguaro in Saguaro National Park-West not far from Tucson has been nicknamed Grandaddy. Rangers have estimated this one cactus to be over 300 years old, and unfortunately it is now dying.

The saguaro has a skeleton of seventeen to twenty-eight upright and long ribs supporting it. A slow-growing plant, it first begins developing branches around age seventy-five. While most saguaros have five to six arms, some have as many as fifty. The saguaro is one of those cacti with a taproot, but it may go only as deep as two to three feet underground. Most of its roots extend around the plant in a thirty-five to fifty foot radius. This root system allows one saguaro plant to absorb as much as a ton of water during

Saguaro cactus can grow up to 60 feet tall and live over 200 years. It doesn't begin to grow arms until it's about 75 years old. This mature saguaro now towers over its nurse tree. Its fruit grows at the ends of the arms. (Photo courtesy of Kevilee Schaich)

desert storms. It also keeps the density in a saguaro forest at about twenty plants per acre.

The plant doesn't begin blooming until age sixty. It takes more than that to start growing arms. Saguaro flowers begin to bloom in mid-May. The blooms open so high off the ground that they're difficult for us ground-huggers to see well. While doves and bees help themselves to the nectar and spread pollen at the same time, bats are a saguaro's primary pollinators.

Saguaro blossoms open around midnight and die the next afternoon, living less than twenty-four hours. Deceptively fragile in appearance, the pure white petals are strong enough to hold a bat's weight while it licks up the nectar, dusting its nose and face with the pollen and carrying it on to the next bloom.

The saguaro has long been a source of sustenance to both man and beast in the desert. The blooms become fruit, quickly ripening mid-to late June. If unharvested by human hands, they split open to display black seeds against a bright red background. This bright red fruit is mistaken by some for red flowers.

This fruit plays an important part in the lives of the Tohono O'odham people. For centuries they have used long, L-shaped poles made from saguaro ribs and a mesquite branch to knock down the fruit. The sweet pulp is scooped out and boiled down to a syrup. This in turn is fermented into a wine used during the Tohono O'odham New Year ceremonies (usually the last few days of June) that bring on the summer rains.

Many desert animals have learned to use the saguaros. Saguaros become condominiums. The Gila woodpecker and other birds break through the tough skin and hollow out spaces for their nests. The holes that are made, "saguaro boots," callus over inside the cactus, and serve as nesting sites for generations of birds. Doves, wrens, flickers, and thrashers feast off the nectar of the saguaro blooms.

Please remember that the saguaro is an endangered plant. Damaging, destroying, or removing one is unlawful. Plants, animals, and even rocks hauled out of the mountains, destroy the natural beauty for all. Leave the beauty of the desert intact for the next passerby.

Cholla—Don't Hug the Teddybear

There are numerous varieties of cholla, but a very common one around Tucson is the teddy bear cholla, distinguished by its heavy coating of spines. Its general shape and profusion of spines make the cactus segments look just like innocent teddy bears covered with a soft, plush fur. The authors do not recommend hugging teddy bear cactus—or any other kind, for that matter.

While cholla spines differ in length from one variety to another, all are surrounded by the tiny glochid spines and share the barb at the tip. Teddy bear's cousin, the jumping cholla, is found almost exclusively around Tucson.

Be careful that you aren't introduced to "jumping cactus" the wrong way. This cactus earns its name because it seems to jump out at you if you come too close. Small jointed segments of the plant form a base for long, curved thorns. Each segment is fully coated with bristling spines and attached very loosely to the mother plant. The slightest brush of skin or clothing against or even near one makes a segment "jump" off the plant and onto you.

Prickly Pear

Like the cholla, there are a lot of different types of prickly pear. Some are purple, some have elongated pads, some seem not even to have spines (don't believe it).

Prickly pears bloom in bright yellows, oranges, and pinks. After the blooms fade, fruit forms and continues to ripen well into September. Tasting slightly sweet, with a hint of cucumber or watermelon, the pears are used in jams and jellies.

The thorns appear to be quite long and fairly well separated. But look closer at prickly pear fruit and you see numerous little round patches scattered around the outside. They're groups of a myriad of thorns, very tiny, very sharp, very thin, and very eager to puncture your skin. Each little patch is called a glochid.

Not only is the prickly pear fruit edible, so are the pads. They're called nopales and taste like slightly peppery green beans. They've been an important green vegetable in this area for a long time. Today they're also eaten pickled or added to a number of main dishes. In late April or early May, when immature pads are about as big as a silver dollar, they are scraped, rinsed, and added raw to salads. Larger, more mature pads are parboiled after cleaning and used whole or in strips.

To try either of these (sans prickles) check the local supermarket. Pads are available fresh in the produce section, as well as canned or pickled. Fresh pears may be up to three inches long. Cut one in half and eat hearty, seeds and all, using a spoon. Prickly pear jam or jelly is also commercially available.

Organ Pipe

The organ pipe cactus is most common in Mexico. North of the border, its habitat is limited to about 500 square miles centered in the Sonoran Desert. Resembling small and thin saguaro cacti clustered together, a single plant can grow as high as twenty-five feet. The Organ Pipe Cactus National Monument near Ajo west of Tucson has a wonderful drive around Ajo Mountain. It showcases not only organ pipe cacti, but twenty-nine other species of cacti and animals found nowhere else in the United States.

Barrel Cactus

The barrel cactus, of which there are several varieties, looks at first glance like a saguaro cactus that never grew. But there are distinct differences. They're easiest to tell apart in the spring. Saguaros have to be at least seventy-five years old before their stark white flowers appear. If you see a short cactus with yellow, orange, or pink flowers, it's a barrel cactus.

Is this a barrel cactus or a young saguaro? A young saguaro. They tend to grow taller and skinnier than their barrel-shaped cousin.

Incidentally, because the barrel cactus can withstand drought conditions longer than most other cacti, it is also called the "water barrel." You've undoubtedly seen at least one Western movie where people are saved from dying of thirst by drinking fluid squeezed from cactus pulp. Well, don't try this at home. The fluid in most cacti is at least distasteful, and at most potentially deadly. The fluid in some cacti varieties contains alkaloids.

Century Plant

Strictly speaking, the century plant isn't a cactus. It's an agave, a succulent native to desert regions. Some varieties of agave produce a fiber called false sisal, used for cording. The sap of another variety is fermented to produce pulque, the basis of the liquor mescal. The century plant is the best known of this group. Tipped with respectable spikes and with thorned edges, these plants are most known for their singular flowering habit.

The so-called century plant is reputed to live for 100 years, and to bloom only once before dying. Half-right. It does bloom only once, and a spectacular sight it is. However, it doesn't always live 100 years. So the century plant perks along for as many decades as it can eke out in the hot, cruel desert. When it feels the call of the beyond, it puts forth one final effort. A stalk unlike any other the plant has grown before emerges from the very center of the plant. Looking for all the world like an asparagus stalk on steroids, it climbs up as far as the plant can manage, often twenty feet or more. Once fully extended, what looked like flaps begin to unfold and smaller stalks branch out.

Eventually the flowers dry up and seeds form, and the stalk dries as the plant below it withers. All its strength went into creating the stalk, and now its job is done. Once it has completed the flowering process, the main plant dies. If you look around the base, however, you may find miniature daughter plants willing to develop into new plants.

The plant may also be grown from seeds, bulbs, or under-ground stems.

A full-grown (adequately watered) century plant can occupy a circular area ten feet or more in diameter. Their V-shaped leaves can extend six feet and are tipped with sharp thorns.

A century plant in full bloom. The stalk is about 30 feet high and over a foot thick at its base. Notice the large group of spikes surrounding the base. On top of the house across the street is an evaporative (swamp) cooler.

Ocotillo

Not a cactus but a shrub, the ocotillo is a rather stringy-looking plant. Branching from a common root and growing eight to twelve feet high, in the spring bright red flowers at the tip of each branch attract hummingbirds.

If you look closely at ocotillo branches, each branch is covered with some very intense thorns. As with cacti, these thorns keep hungry desert dwellers from munching out on the plant. The branches may or may not contain leaves, as leaves appear only after it's rained, and then not even on all ocotillos.

The ocotillo is a great plant for fencing. Remember, however, desert plants are very hardy, so fencing with ocotillo can lead to a surprise. To make an ocotillo fence, simply chop the branches to the desired length plus enough to stick into the ground. Usually a heavy-gauge wire is anchored to a rebar or other heavy stake and woven horizontally through the branches at different heights to keep the fence upright. One fine spring day after the winter rains, however, you might check the fence and find it's sprouting leaves. You now have a living ocotillo fence!

Wildflowers

There are other desert plants besides cactus. Because of the high heat and lack of water, many of our wildflowers are smaller than you'd find under more favorable conditions.

When winter rains have been generous, spring is a glorious celebration of color. Wildflowers tend to grow in large fields so that in some areas the desert is carpeted by blooms in every shade of the rainbow. Desert mallows, poppies, lupines and daisies, brittlebush and fiddleneck, Mexican gold poppies, owl clovers, and desert bluebells are just a few of the plants you may see.

Desert plants are choosy, though. Wildflower seeds may lie dormant for years waiting for just the right conditions. Different flowers bloom at different times during the season, and the site of flowers in bloom changes from week to week.

You can find which locations are in bloom by checking the *Arizona Daily Star*. During the spring it prints a "Wildflower Watch" that lists locations of wildflower displays. There's also a Wildflower Hotline number (602/418-8134—this is a Phoenix number, not toll-free) maintained by the Desert Botanical Garden. Updated every Friday, it gives information on wildflower locations state-wide.

Trees

At many of Tucson's fine steakhouses, you'll no doubt see the term "mesquite-broiled." Mesquite is a gnarly, rough-barked tree with delicate leaves, nasty spines (what else?), and bean pods. Early settlers in the region ground the mesquite beans for flour, and today they are sometimes used for animal feed. The tree grows up to thirty feet tall and provides wispy shade under its rather large crown. A true desert plant, mesquite roots have been noted by miners as deep as 175 feet underground.

Another tree common in Tucson is the appropriately named (and equally thorny) palo verde (green stick). It was so-named by the Spanish because when it is young the tree looks like just a bunch of green sticks popping out of the ground. As the tree matures, the "sticks" eventually fuse into a single trunk. It grows into a rather short, spindly tree. The green bark is actually another adaptation to the desert climate. Even if it is totally denuded of leaves during a drought, the green bark continues the photosynthesis process and keeps the tree alive.

Plants

Desert broom is a thornless, bushy plant common around Tucson. Actually used by early settlers as a broom, it's one of the first plants to spring up around newly cleared land. In the spring its white blossoms blow down streets like eddies of snow.

Another equally common bush is the creosote. This pungent-smelling woody bush also lacks thorns. Its blossoms are yellow, with a fuzzy white fruit (inedible, incidently) about the size of a raisin.

Once a very common sight along a desert road, the tumbleweed has all but vanished from the landscape. Not native to the Sonoran region, seed of the Russian thistle was introduced into the United States as unwanted stowaways in seed and grain shipments. A green globe when actively growing, the dried plant turns to a straw color and the main stem breaks off close to the ground in autumn.

The bright red-yellow-orange blossoms of the mexican bird of paradise draw attention to this showy desert plant. Like the palm tree, this has become a successful transplant, bringing summer color to Tucson streets. It's a familiar sight, not least because of its frequent incorporation into city landscaping. A native from Mexico that has naturalized around the Tucson area, it has the added advantage of being attractive to butterflies.

Gardening in the Desert

As you might not know, the desert isn't entirely hostile to transplants. From tumbleweed to palm tree, this barren land has proven a welcoming host to all sorts of plants. Unfortunately, in some cases this welcome has backfired. Even before becoming known as a haven for lung-damaged veterans of World War I, doctors sent "lungers" (like Doc

Holliday) to the desert for their health. The dry, clean air gave many a new lease on life.

They did so well here, many decided to stay. But then they decided to "improve" things a bit. To "make it a bit more like home," forgetting that they came here because home was killing them. Before long there were lush green lawns sprouting palm and olive and mulberry trees all over the place. The list grew and grew, and before you knew it the area became known as the "pollen capital" of the world.

In an effort to provide both short- and long-term relief for allergy sufferers, Pima County has banned the planting of olive and mulberry trees. Old ones can stay but can't be replaced. In addition, lawns of Bermuda grass have to be mowed however often is necessary to keep seed heads from forming.

Animals

The Cold-Blooded Side of the Desert

The desert is home to many animals. Some of them are dangerous but others are not. Cold-blooded animals such as lizards and snakes are very common.

The Horned Toad

One of the most common and fearsome looking, yet totally safe animals is the horned toad. For all its fearsomeness, it is quite harmless.

You may be hard pressed to find one, however. They're so incredibly well camouflaged in the desert dirt that it seems like they're invisible. From about an inch to nearly six inches long, horned toads resemble little dinosaurs. Spines and prickles cover their back, and an armored frill protects the vulnerable neck. Not a toad, despite its name, but a lizard, it relies on its coloring for protection. Camouflage and stillness are its forte as a predator.

However, when it is attacked, it has the ability to puff itself up to almost twice its normal size. This prevents predators from swallowing it, and they often let it go once caught. Also, its larger body size can scare off predators.

Horny toad legends say they cry blood. Quite true. When disturbed, it cries tears of "blood" from special organs near its eyes.

As with any reptile it's cold-blooded, and temperature changes can be deadly. To help sense the changes, the horned toad has a "third eye," located on top of its head. When it's too hot or cold, or when frightened, the lizard burrows underneath the desert sand until nothing shows but that one spot on its head. When the temperature is more to its liking or a danger has disappeared, the horned toad climbs back to the surface.

Rattlesnakes

Ask an out-of-state visitor what animal they're most likely to run into in the desert, and "rattlesnake" will probably be mentioned first. Rattlesnakes aren't anything to fool with, but they certainly aren't any reason to avoid the desert. You don't often find one within the city limits anymore. Even out in the desert they're hard to find. They sense you and usually stay out of your way. But you should be aware of the possibility of an encounter.

When walking along trails or climbing rocks, it's a good idea to make some noise. Most animals will avoid you, but they do need to know you are there. Scuffle your feet, particularly when walking near brush. If you hear a rattle, stop. If you can locate it, slowly move away from the snake. If you can't find it, retrace your steps and go back the way you came.

Eleven species of rattlesnakes live in Arizona. This snake is a pit viper, the fastest-striking snake in the world. A skeptical researcher once matched mongeese against a rattler. Yes, plural. Final score was rattlers all, mongeese none. Compared to a rattler, cobras strike in slow motion.

Contrary to popular belief, rattlers don't have to be coiled to strike. They can strike in any direction, at least half the length of their body. Because they use infrared heat sensors to locate prey, they're accurate even in total darkness. Their fangs are as fine as the finest hypodermic needle. They are kept folded up into the roof of their mouth until striking. Because there are several rows of back-up fangs, it only takes two days to replace a broken one.

Even if you're bitten, 25 percent of all bites to humans are "dry" (no venom released). An envenomed bite generally produces symptoms such as pain, swelling, and redness at the site. These symptoms increase and spread with time. DO NOT cut the bite site; DO NOT use a tourniquet; DO NOT give drugs or alcohol—the combination can be fatal; DO NOT pack in ice; DO NOT apply an electrical jolt to the punctures. DO get medical attention A.S.A.P.

Gila Monsters

They aren't too common, but if you see a Gila monster, leave it alone! The Gila (pronounced hee-la) monster is a large, seemingly slow-moving lizard with a tail almost as large as its body. It is the only poisonous lizard found in the U.S. Brightly colored, mixing an orange-yellow color mottled with black, the Gila monster can grow to two feet long. They have a slow and deliberate walk but can whirl to either side in a blink.

Grabbing one by the tail is not recommended, nor is getting close to one. These are shy, solitary creatures and not often seen. You almost have to beg to be bitten by one. If you are bitten, first get the thing to let go (which can be a real problem), and then seek medical attention immediately.

Unlike a rattlesnake, all Gila bites are envenomed. The bite is considered more painful than a rattlesnake, but slightly less toxic. However, no antivenom is available for

Gila venom. Once having bitten they hold on tenaciously, and the longer they bite the more venom is delivered. Experts suggest immersing the lizard in cold water, pushing a stick into its nostril, or prying the mouth open with whatever you have handy. Far better to just leave the Gila alone in the first place. You'll both be happier.

Coyote and Friends

No mention of desert animals is complete without coyote. On the outskirts of the city coyotes are fairly common. The dry washes provide natural pathways for these predators. In spring and early summer, when doors and windows are open to the night air, you can hear coyotes sing their raucous chorus of yips and yaps. One or two of them start with excited, shrill cries, and suddenly the air swells with the combined cries of the pack. They stop just as suddenly as they started, making you wonder just what they're up to.

Coyote is a big player in Native American legends. Coyote is also an enigma. He's both the tormenter and champion of man. He has the reputation of being a good intentioned but terrible trickster, who most often winds up on the short end of the trick.

A Navajo story told of him concerns First Woman. She wanted the laws visible for all to read. First Man suggested placing the laws in the sky, where everyone could see them. First Woman brought out the stars and gathered them in a blanket. Spreading the blanket at her feet, she began placing the stars, one at a time, in careful patterns in the night sky.

Old Man Coyote came along and saw First Woman. When he learned what she was doing, he wanted to help. She accepted his offer, and for a while they worked together. But Coyote was impatient. He couldn't stand the long, slow job. It would take forever at this rate! So he grabbed two corners of the blanket and, whoosh! scattered the stars into the sky, ruining First Woman's careful patterns, but creating the Milky Way.

That is why there is so much confusion in the world today, because coyote mixed up the laws.

In absolute fairness to coyote, however, there's another version of how he placed the stars in the sky. The Wasco Indian legend tells how Old Man Coyote, an excellent archer, used arrows to build himself a ladder to the moon. Climbing up, he stood on the moon and used still more arrows, shifting the stars around in the sky to form patterns. When the stars were arranged to his liking, he climbed back down his arrow-ladder.

Once back in the desert, Coyote sang at the moon until all his animal friends came to see why he was calling them. "Look up," he told them. "I've placed you all in the skies." The birds and animals looked up and were amazed to see their likenesses traced with stars in the night sky.

The Wascos use this story to explain why coyote howls at the night sky: so all can take note of his handiwork.

You may not meet up with Old Man Coyote, but around Tucson an encounter with a coyote isn't unlikely. Looking something like a devolved German shepherd, coyotes are very successful predators and scavengers. It's no big deal for a coyote to scale a fence, snatch up a cat or small dog, and jump right back out again.

Social, gregarious animals, their yip-yip-yip greetings and calls are frequently heard in the evenings. If you do see one or more, you'll notice that while they avoid you, they don't display any fear.

Black Bear

The black bear is a year-round resident of the upper reaches of the Catalina Mountains. Unfortunately, as in many national parks and other wilderness areas that have been encroached upon by man, the black bear is losing the war. Once a bear becomes accustomed to man's presence, about the first thing he learns is that man brings food. From garbage can to table scraps to picnic cooler, signs of food are quickly recognized. Bears have been known to break and peel windows out of a car to reach a cooler visible on the back seat, so be aware.

Unfortunately, knowingly or not, in most cases the lesson is taught to the bears by visitors who feed them. This is doubly unfortunate because it not only places the humans in jeopardy, it's a virtual death sentence for the bear. A bear who learns to associate people with food eventually will invade campsites, looking for something to eat. This behavior eventually brings them into conflict with humans, and in such encounters the bear is always the loser. While relocation is the first option, a bear who returns to the scene of previous crimes rarely survives the experience.

If you go up to Mt. Lemmon or any other destination in the Catalinas, don't have food out unless you're eating. Bears aren't that common, but there's no reason to risk it. Don't leave food out on your table or in your tent. If you've packed in food, hang it over a tree limb. Make sure it's not only high enough off the ground, but far enough from the trunk to be out of a bear's reach. If you can touch it, it's too close. Hide coolers, backpacks, etc. in your trunk, or at least throw a blanket over them in the back seat. If you're camping overnight, while it sounds sort of funny, don't let your kids have food in their tent or go to bed with food on their faces. That warm washcloth that wakes them up could be a bear's tongue.

Wings in the Desert

Hummingbirds

The desert is home to many creatures, and they're not all snakes or lizards. Watching hummingbirds is better than watching television. While many of these winged jewels make Tucson their home on a year-round basis, Tucson is also on the migratory route for a number of hummingbird species.

The Anna's hummingbird is perhaps the most common. It has a glistening red crown and throat, outdoing the eastern ruby-throated hummingbird one better. Other hummingbirds that visit feeders are Costas, broad-tailed, and blue-throated hummingbirds.

The Arizona Sonoran Desert Museum has a hummingbird sanctuary with many species. If you prefer to see hummingbirds in large numbers in the wild, up close and personal, take the drive to Madera Canyon, south of Tucson (see page 178 for directions). There are a number of hummingbird feeders strategically placed near the lodge. Just about every variety of hummingbird in Arizona eventually shows up to feed, sometimes as many as six at the same feeder. Bring binoculars for even more spectacular viewing!

Cactus Wren

Many birds make Tucson their home. The cactus wren is Arizona's state bird. It's a saucy bird, not above chasing cats or even people who stray too close to a nesting site. The cactus wren has a variety of calls and is quite common. It has a distinctive reddish cap, separated from the rest of its head by a white band above the eye. Brown dashed markings line up along its body, clustering at the adult's throat, but run horizontally across its tail.

Mockingbird

The northern mockingbird resembles the cactus wren, if only in actions. A quick-moving, perky bird about the same size as the wren, its ability to imitate other's calls doesn't help pin it down. It's easiest to distinguish in flight, when its white wing patches are visible.

Phainopepla

Another bird with white wing patches only visible in flight is the Phainopepla. The male of these slender crested birds is all black and the female a sooty charcoal grey, but when they fly they display their white wing markings.

Woodpeckers

The Gila woodpecker and the ladder-backed woodpecker look very much alike in their black and white feathers. The markings of both resemble the rungs of a ladder going up their backs. You can tell them apart by the red head the male Gila woodpecker sports. It's also a much larger bird than the ladder-backed.

Cardinals

Those who think of the red-robed cardinal as a bird of the northern climes may be surprised to learn that it thrives here. The male is a very bright red with black accents, while the female displays a more muted orange to dusky-grey coat.

Doves

Doves are ubiquitous in the desert. Three varieties are commonly seen in the Tucson area. The large rock dove (a.k.a. feral pigeon) is grey with black wing bars, and he and his cousins the pigeons are everywhere. The mourning dove is a slightly smaller bird than the rock Dove, brown to the rock's grey. They're easily told apart in the air, as the rock dove spreads its fantail wide while the mourning dove's tail is pointed. The Inca dove is a very small bird, reddish brown and speckled. When flying, the Inca's wings display a distinct red tinge.

Roadrunner

Then there's the roadrunner, clown of the desert. You've surely seen him depicted in cartoons. It is quite a large bird, with a colorful green-red-white streak just behind its eye that shows only when the sun catches it just right. When it runs it stretches its long neck out and balances and steers with its lengthy tail, a mottled brown and cream streak across the desert. While perfectly capable of flying, he prefers racing over the desert floor on foot. A member of the cuckoo family, roadrunner eggs are laid in a shallow depression scooped in the dirt. Once hatched, the chicks are on their own fairly quickly and come into their full two-foot length in their second year.

Quail

Another amusing desert bird is the Gambel's quail. It has a small, black plume of feathers that curves over its dark-red forehead like an art deco headdress. Quail chicks stick around mom and dad for quite a while, almost literally. It's amusing watching these birds and their chicks. They run across the ground one right after the other, practically stepping in each others' footsteps. They almost never move in a straight line, but rather in short S-curved patterns. Watching a quail family in transit is like watching a miniature choo-choo train powered by rapidly moving pairs of feet.

In the mountains, particularly the Catalinas, you may also catch sight of the mountain quail, easily distinguishable from the Gambel's by its upright head plume. In addition, the mountain quail has a grey forehead and chestnut throat instead of the black forehead and throat of the Gambel's.

Owls

The night has wings. Great horned owls are not uncommon. Burrowing owls are also common in the desert, but you have to pay attention to see them. Fairly small for an owl but with relatively long legs, they prefer open areas where they can see what's coming. They're most often spotted standing on fence-posts or some other vantage point. While they can dig their own burrows, they commonly take over those dug and abandoned by coyotes or badgers. They've also been known to occupy a prairie dog or ground squirrel den (generally after eating the former inhabitant).

If you see a truly tiny owl, say six inches or so—you've found either the elf or (Ferruginous) pigmy owl. Brown and cream, they look pretty much alike.

Raptors and Scavengers

It's quite common to see very large birds circling at various elevations high over the desert. Turn your eyes skyward on hot days and you can see them gliding, hardly moving a wing. Hot air rises from the desert in swirls called thermals. These thermals create an elevator to higher levels for sailing birds. Many of the larger birds of prey use these thermals to conserve energy while moving up high for a good view.

Ravens and turkey vultures are the scavengers of the desert. The turkey vulture's naked red head and curved bill make it easy to identify, as long as you can make out the head. Ravens also ride the thermals, and while they're large they don't quite match the vulture's six-foot wingspan.

Hawks are also found in abundance in our desert, among them red-tailed and Cooper's. An occasional peregrine falcon may be seen, or perhaps an Aplomado falcon visiting from Mexico. They all take advantage of the free ride thermals provide at one time or another.

Because Tucson is so close to the Mexico border, we have the opportunity of seeing birds that don't make an appearance much further north. Lucky visitors to Madera Canyon may catch sight of an elegant trogon, one of the most colorful birds in the world.

To learn more about the rich variety of bird life in the desert, Tohono Chul Park (see page 152) offers guided bird walks. These begin in early morning when it's cool and last until about lunchtime, when you can take a break in their tearoom.

Other Tucson Wildlife

Because Tucson is in large part a rural community, it's not uncommon for those living on the outskirts to see deer, javalina (a wild pig, also called peccary), jackrabbits, and other wildlife walking unconcernedly through their yards. If you take time to explore some of the many trails in the mountains around Tucson, you'll probably see them yourself. One caution, however: Remember these are wild animals. They're not in a zoo; they live free and do what they know works, in an environment they were born to. Leave them alone, give them distance, and they'll be around for a long time for everyone to enjoy.

If you happen across what seems like an abandoned wild baby, the best thing you can do is leave it alone. Many desert animals depend on camouflage to protect the young. The babies stay still so they can't be seen by predators. The well-meaning person who "rescues" a wild animal may actually be condemning it. The parent may even be within sight, but hidden from you. Leave the little ones alone. Give the mother time to return and find her babies unharmed.

If you do find an injured animal or babies who are truly abandoned, place them in a box lined with a soft cloth or towel. Handle them as little as possible. This minimizes their becoming accustomed to people and enhances their chance for eventual release. Call the Tucson Wildlife Rehabilitation Council at 792-3947 for instructions on what to do. Resist the temptation to feed animals you find. The most common mistake people make with birds is trying to force-feed them milk. Birds are lactose intolerant, and milk can sicken or kill them.

The Creepy-Crawlies

Scorpions

Nighttime brings out scorpions, nocturnal hunters that they are. The large, hairy ones are the attention-getters, but the really dangerous member of the family is a runt, the "bark" scorpion. Roughly two inches long, slender of tail, straw-colored and nearly translucent, the bark's sting is particularly hazardous for small children. In general, however, scorpion stings are painful but rarely require hospitalization.

Spiders and Centipedes

Two other desert citizens who are both victims of bad press are the tarantula and the desert centipede. The tarantula makes a good monster—big, fat, and hairy. In fact, however, you'd need to pick one up and handle it to get bitten. If you are, the biggest threat you face is infection if the bite isn't cleaned properly.

These large arachnids live in ground burrows, which are distinguishable from the burrow of any other creature only by the silken web just inside the entrance. They're not usually seen during the day unless it's really cloudy and overcast, or if their burrow gets flooded during a rainstorm. Some people like to having a tarantula around, because they're great insect hunters—others prefer the bugs.

The desert does have its complement of venomous spiders. The black widow lives here, as does a cousin of the better known brown recluse, the Arizona brown spider. A bite from either of these represents a much more serious threat than the tarantula. Both seem to hide in places people stick their fingers without looking.

The presence of a black widow is often noted because its webs are extremely sticky and fairly strong. Its venom affects large muscle groups, and an adult who has been bitten is advised to take pain medication (Tylenol, aspirin) and either to soak the bite in a warm tub or to use ice packs. Seek medical help if the pain becomes too severe or if you begin to have an allergic reaction to the bite such as shortness of breath or wheezing.

Victims of the much rarer Arizona brown spider often don't realize they've been bitten until as long as forty-eight hours afterward. The Arizona brown's venom is necrotizing, meaning it kills tissue. It is also extremely painful. If it looks like a dark brown or black center is developing in the center of a very painful lump, seek medical assistance!

The desert centipede can grow more than a foot long and has forty-two legs, one pair per segment, but like the tarantula it's mainly a victim of its image. Its bite is about as painful as a bee sting, and there may be some localized swelling, but it usually isn't serious. Make sure you clean any bite well, and always feel free to seek medical attention.

"Killer" Bees

The last few years have seen a little hysteria on the subject of "killer" bees, or Africanized honey bees. In South America in the 1950s, an African queen bee that was being used for research was accidentally released. She lived and thrived, and swarms of her progeny headed north. These hybrids crossed the Mexican border in 1993. The difference between the Africanized bees and the European honey bee (the common variety) is in temperament. These insects have a really rotten attitude and attack in swarms, stinging without stopping.

The best thing to do is to stay away from all bees. If you see bees, don't get close; Africanized bees are differentiated from honey bees only under a microscope. They take any incursion into their territory as a threat, and the entire hive comes out on the offensive.

If you are attacked, the best defense is to run like blazes! They tend to go for the head, so cover your face if you can without slowing down and get inside as fast as possible—a car, house, outhouse, anywhere you can keep the rest of the swarm away while doing in the ones that arrive with you.

The desert has its complement of insects, but like its weather, unhappy encounters aren't that common. Tucson is not a "buggy" city. Except for mosquitoes in certain areas, there are few truly pestiferous types around. If you run across a truly humongous bug, it's probably a Palo Verde beetle. It looks big enough to fly away with you, but it's harmless.

Mountains, Canyons, and Caves

Once you're prepared for the heat, your eyes automatically focus on our natural skyline. The mountain ranges are the largest points of reference in Tucson. The valley floor was formed by the erosion from these mountains over the millennia. The plants and animals that have adapted their lifestyle to the desert call it their home.

Tucson is ringed with mountains. To the north, up close, are the Catalina Mountains. Move around to the southeast and you can see how the Tanque Verde range connects them to the Rincons, much lower and rounder, Tucson's eastern border. The Santa Rita Mountains are far enough away to the south so that you can't see much of their features easily, mostly just their silhouette against the sky. The Tucson

Mountain range is led by "A" Mountain, marching back from downtown Tucson. It depends on your vantage point, but for the most part they're just high enough to be noticeable on the horizon but leaving a lot of sky above them. Since there are very few places in Tucson from which no mountains are visible, it's easy to orient yourself by which mountain range you're facing.

Of course, the mountains have other advantages than just helping locate north. They provide our local wildlife with a diversity of environments, and each range has multiple destinations for travelers. They add to the natural beauty of the area. And it's thanks to the mountains that we have such an abundance of hiking and biking opportunities around Tucson. Once you begin enjoying Tucson's mountains, you'll be happy to learn that much of the area is protected. Tucson Mountain Park, Coronado National Forest, Saguaro National Park, Pusch Ridge Wilderness Area—all are protected areas. Please treat our natural areas with respect to assures that these resources remain for all to enjoy.

Rincon Mountains

The sun rises over the Rincon Mountains, directly east of the city. The Rincons define the eastern boundary of the Tucson Valley. While the Catalina Highway goes over the Catalinas, no roads cross through the Rincon Mountains. These 58,000 acres of wilderness, however, crowned by Tanque Verde Peak, Rincon Peak, and Mica Mountain (8,666 feet), do provide hikers and backpackers with any number of trails to choose from. Saguaro National Park-East takes in a substantial area of the range, and Colossal Cave runs beneath it even further south. There are many hiking trails, and the rather low elevation attracts many. Be aware, though, that there are a variety of different trails with varying degrees of difficulty.

The Rincons are easy to get to; just drive east all the way down Speedway Boulevard. It may sound far, but it's only about a ten-minute drive from Kolb Road or thereabouts. A trail head lies just beyond the end of Speedway, where the road branches to the left into the Tanque Verde Guest Ranch. Straight ahead are the Rincons and an unofficial entrance to Saguaro National Park-East. There's a parking lot on the right, but if it's full, you can park along the road. There are signs that point out the various trails and their directions. Follow the trail that appeals to you the most.

Saguaro National Park-East was Saguaro National Monument until being designated a national park in 1994, and occupies ninety-nine square miles of the Rincons. (The West unit is on the other side of the valley, past the Tucson Mountains.) The official ranger station, visitor center, and entrance is on Old Spanish Trail Road, south of Broadway Avenue.

Cactus Forest Drive is a nine-mile loop through the saguaro forest in Saguaro National Park-East. It provides a scenic introduction to this unique cactus, as well as to much of the other vegetation common to the Sonoran desert. The fortunate visitor may also catch a glimpse of some of our wildlife, from javalina, bobcat, and coyote to snakes and lizards. Don't forget to look up! Hawks and buzzards are on the lookout, too.

For those who would like both a closer view and a clue, a wheelchair accessible walkway has been created. Plants are labeled so you can tell what that funny-looking thing really is. There are also guided tours, as well as regular programs and presentations.

To get here, take Old Spanish Trail about five miles east from the intersection of Broadway and Old Spanish Trail. There's a visitor center at the entrance, with exhibits and dioramas.

Colossal Cave is located southeast of Tucson, on the south face of the Rincon Mountains. (See page 119 for more information.)

The Catalinas and Rincons run into each other, forming Tucson's far northeast corner. The dividing line runs through Agua Caliente Hill. This is the peak just to the north of Redington Road (Tanque Verde Road), the route through Redington Pass to the towns of Redington and San Manuel.

Santa Catalina Mountains

The Catalinas define the north edge of Tucson, with homes being built right up into their foothills. Until a decade or so ago, most if not all of Tucson lay directly south of the mountains. In recent years with its increasing population, Tucson now spills past the Catalinas to their west and north. Upscale subdivisions fill the lower portion of the south-facing foothills. Several world-class resorts (Westin La Paloma, Westward Look, Loew's Ventana Canyon, etc.) dot the smaller canyons along their ridges. Homes are custom-built and carefully oriented to take full advantage of the extraordinary views of city and mountains.

The Catalinas are so close to Tucson that they may appear to be more a very large wall than a mountain range. They rise in a fairly abrupt fashion from the desert floor but continue north and east a considerable distance. If you hike through the area, you may find mortars used by members of the Hohokam or Pima tribes a thousand years ago, or petroglyphs reaching across the gap of time. The Catalinas provided campsites to raiding Apaches, and gold, silver, and copper miners who ventured into the range.

The Santa Catalina Mountains furnish hikers, wildlife enthusiasts, mountain bikers, geology and paleontology students, and those who just simply appreciate their beauty some of the best the Tucson area has to offer. Home to Pusch Ridge Wilderness Area, Mount Lemmon, and Pima, Sabino, and Bear Canyons, the Catalinas could be a full-time occupation for a determined pleasure-seeker.

Looking directly at the face of the Catalinas from Tucson, a great rocky ledge cuts diagonally across their face. This is Pusch Ridge, now a national wilderness area, created in 1978 under the Endangered American Wilderness Act. Nearly all of the southern face of the Catalina Mountain range, almost 57,000 acres, is closed to future development and all motor-driven vehicles. The use of mountain bikes is forbidden, as well. Pusch Ridge is home to some of the last bighorn sheep in the Southwest. Because of their protected status (they're fast becoming scarce) hiking with pets is restricted here. Even with its protected status, human encroachment has sharply curtailed the number of bighorns seen in recent years.

The Catalinas offer several recreational options, of which Sabino Canyon is perhaps the most popular. Inside this federally protected area are numerous hiking trails leading into the mountains. Northeast of town and just inside the foothills, Sabino Canyon is an excellent introduction to our desert mountains.

Even if you are not a hiker, drive up to the foothills anyway. You are never totally away from civilization, and the views of the city and the valley to the south are fantastic.

Tucson Mountains

Almost everyone who comes to Tucson notices (or has pointed out to them) "A" Mountain. "A" Mountain is Sentinel Peak, clearly visible on the west side of the city. The big "A" is whitewashed every fall by incoming freshmen at the University of Arizona.

The Tucson Mountains are those dark, sawtoothed mountains to the west. Gate's Pass in this range, besides being a great spot to watch sunsets, is the gateway to Old Tucson and the Arizona-Sonoran Desert Museum. These are popular attractions for visitors as well as locals. (In an unscientific poll, the Arizona-Sonoran Desert Museum is a

"A" Mountain, as it is now known, was once Sentinel Mountain, where a lookout was kept posted to spot hostile Indians.

"must-see," followed closely by Old Tucson. Since that poll, however, there was a fire at Old Tucson and much of it was damaged.)

Those sites, incidentally, are located within Tucson Mountain Park. Butting right up against Tucson's west flank are the 17,000 acres of Tucson Mountain Park. Its western edge marks the eastern boundary of Saguaro National Park-West. It features miles of hiking and riding trails. There are several picnic sites and a campground.

> ❑ Be aware that day-use sites are closed (locked off) at 10:00 p.m. This means if you pull in to watch the sunset and decide to take a moonlight walk, you could come back and find you can't get out until the next morning.

Old Tucson is about a fifteen-minute drive out into the desert on Gates Pass Road (Speedway Boulevard) from the

I-10 freeway. Continue on about another five minutes to arrive at the Arizona-Sonoran Desert Museum.

Another five minutes brings you to Saguaro National Park-West, the alter ego of Saguaro National Park-East, found across the valley in the Rincon Mountains. Upgraded to national park status in 1994, Saguaro National Park-West is a twenty-four-square-mile site with a much younger saguaro forest. Many of the saguaro you'll see there are still growing under "nurse" trees, palo verde or mesquite trees that provide the young seedlings with shade and protection.

The Bajada Loop Drive inside Saguaro National Park-West is six miles long. As you pass the canyon walls, keep a sharp eye out for Indian pictographs. It also brings you past two of the picnic areas. Four more picnic areas are scattered down the twelve-mile dirt road. All have ramadas for shade over the tables, and grills. Restroom facilities are also furnished.

There is no water available, however. Bring along plenty of water. If you want to bar-b-que, bring your own firewood or charcoal. This is a protected area. You may not remove anything, and that includes deadwood. "Take nothing but memories, leave nothing but footprints."

The park also has self-guided trails, one of which has wheelchair access, as well as over sixteen miles of hiking trails open to the public. Remember your hat and sunscreen, and take more water than you think you'll need.

Santa Rita Mountains

The Santa Rita Mountains are the mountain range wa-a-a-y off to the south of Tucson, about a forty-minute drive on I-19. Rich in gold and silver, these mountains have attracted treasure-hunters since the silver strike there in 1736. The mission at Tumacacori furnished the mines with Indian laborers, with protection provided by the presidio in Tubac. At least they did until the mid-1800s, when repeated Apache attacks forced the mission, presidio, and mines to be abandoned. Mount Wrightson (9,453 feet) and Mount Hopkins bear the names of two men killed by Apaches while they were attempting to survey the mountain range.

If you do any hiking or look at a map of the Santa Ritas, you'll see dozens of mines marked. Most of them were played out by the early 1900s. Helvetia and Greaterville, large towns of 400 and 500 respectively, were at their peak in the 1880s. Today they're ghost towns, and all that remains of the mines are tailings. Careful, many abandoned mines, unmarked holes in the ground, are old and potentially dangerous.

Today the Santa Ritas are part of the Coronado National Forest and a national wilderness area. While this is the furthest range from Tucson, there are numerous hiking trails that allow the visitor entry into these beautiful mountains. Many of them originate from Madera Canyon, and several routes can be combined to create a unique hiking experience.

These four mountain ranges provide the setting for Tucson. Appreciating the jewel of the desert may involve getting into the Southwestern experience.

CHAPTER THREE

The Southwestern Experience

The Hohokam were the first people known to have settled in the Tucson area. Less well known than the Anasazi, traces of the Hohokam civilization extend over nearly 2,000 years of southern Arizona history (circa 300 B.C. to A.D. 1450). Expert farmers, growing maize, beans, squash, and cotton, they built hundreds of miles of canals to irrigate their crops. Their culture diminished in the mid-1400s, and many archeologists believe their descendants comprise today's Pima and O'odham tribes.

If you hike through the Tucson Mountains, you may notice row after row of carefully constructed rock terrace walls. Most noticeable on Tumamoc Hill, the peak behind "A" Mountain, thousands of terraces wind their way across hillslopes in a 125-mile arc. These are miscalled *trincheras* (trenches), although from a distance they do resemble fortifications. So far no authentic dating has been made, nor is it truly known if they were used for farming, living or—as their appearance suggests—defense.

Cowboys and Indians, good guys and bad guys, gunfights and sheriffs—or at least movies' and television's version of them—have all shaped our expectations of what the West was like.

In a city with the history and background of Tucson, you wouldn't expect to be far removed from the Western experience. Much to our own surprise, while doing research for this book, we found that the movies aren't always that far off from what things were like and what really happened on a day-to-day basis. In many instances the movies under-report the conditions of the times and the hard existence living on the frontier entailed.

Tucson isn't in just the West, it's in the Southwest. The Southwest adds quite a number of flavors to the pot, so to speak, with the influence of Mexico and the Southwestern Indians. Stir these ingredients together with the westward expansion of the United States and you're bound to find some interesting results. The United States is the melting pot of the world. Tucson is the melting pot of the Southwest.

Tucsonans do recognize where they live for what it is. It's a hard place. Always has been. Live here for more than a year and you'll know that. If it weren't for modern technology, communication, amenities, and conveniences, the desert would be a very difficult place to live. A favorite saying "But it's a dry heat!" isn't enough to overcome the heat of a hot summer. So Tucsonans poke fun at themselves.

You have to have a sense of humor to live in the desert. If it's that way now, think of what it must have been like 100 or so years ago. Then, just as now, you had to have a sense of humor. The following "poem" was composed by Charles O. Brown of Tucson in the 1870s. It gets the idea across pretty well:

ARIZONA
How It Was Made and Who Made It

The devil was given permission one day
To select him a land for his own special sway;
So he hunted around for a month or more,
And fussed and fumed and terribly swore.
But at last was delighted a country to view
Where the prickly pear and mesquite grew.
With a survey brief, without further excuse,
He stood on the banks of the Santa Cruz.

He saw there were some improvements to make,
For he felt his own reputation at stake.
An idea struck him, and he swore by his horns
To make a complete vegetation of thorns.
He studded the land with the prickly pear,
And scattered the cactus everywhere:
The Spanish dagger, sharp-pointed and tall,
And at last the chollas to outstick them all.
He imported the Apaches directly from Hell,
With a legion of skunks, with a loud, loud smell
To perfume the country he loved so well.
And then for his life he couldn't see why
The river need any more water supply,
And he swore if he gave it another drop
You might have his head and horns for a mop.
He filled the river with sand till 'twas almost dry,
And poisoned the land with alkali;
And promised himself on its slimy brink
To control all who from it would drink.
He saw there was one improvement to make,
So he imported the scorpion, tarantula, and snake.
That all that might come to this country to dwell
Would be sure to think it was almost Hell,
He fixed the heat at a hundred and 'leven
And banished forever the moisture from Heaven;
And remarked as he heard his furnaces roar,
That the heat might reach five hundred or more:
And after he fixed things so thorny and well,
He said: "I'll be damned if this don't beat Hell."
Then he flapped his wings and away he flew
And vanished from earth in a blaze of blue.

(Charles O. Brown, quoted from *Helldorado*, William M. Breakenridge, University of Nebraska Press, 1992)

It wasn't just the desert and the weather that made living hard. The people who lived here, and the circumstances under which they lived, were also hard. Mr. Brown, whose doggerel is quoted above, was originally a bounty hunter. For what was he paid a bounty? Indian scalps. Not necessarily the nicest man you'd like to know, but he eventually settled in Tucson in 1861. He built "Congress Hall," the best saloon in southern Arizona. The early political meetings in the Arizona Territory were held there because it was the best (read only) place available.

One of the greatest precipitants of change in the Southwest was the horse, followed closely by cattle. In 1519, when the Spanish invaded Mexico, they brought both horses and cattle with them. The horse had existed in the Americas in previous ages, but it was a smaller version and had become extinct long ago. Cattle were entirely new to this continent. In the late 1800s, over the three centuries since their introduction, horses and cattle had been adopted into the everyday lives of Mexicans and North American Indians, and with them spread northward into what is now the United States.

In the earliest days there was little commercial use for these horses and cows. Except for the very important use as food and for transportation and work, there was no large commercial use for them. They were still a very important commodity, and an unending and inviting attraction for raiding Apaches.

But as the commercial outlets for horses and beef developed, the horse moved into its own. When the ranching industry took off, cattle and horses became common throughout the area. The quarter horse dates back to 1792. During the nation's westward expansion it made its mark on American history.

In the nineteenth century the horse was the cowboy's jeep. Cowboys were the ranch employees responsible for the transportation (cattle drives) of the herds to market, and for breaking (training) the wild horses. Because the demand for food far outweighed the demand for transportation, the ranch industry raised many more cattle than horses. But horses were essential both for the raising of cattle and for traveling the long distances necessary to move the cattle to market. Horses eventually were the essential means for moving through the desert. So we link the word "cowboy" with the desert.

The discovery of gold in California brought an increased interest in cattle to Arizona. Prices for beef were driven up to feed the mad scrabble of people who were rushing to California. Cattle were driven west from Texas through Arizona to California where they sold for as much as $100 a head.

The first ranch in the Tucson area was the Canoa Ranch, on the Santa Cruz River about thirty-five miles south. William Oury, first mayor of Tucson, started a ranch just south of Tucson. He later moved to Tanque Verde, an area of Pima County that is a "suburb" of Tucson. Raiding Apache Indians caused many ranches to fail. It wasn't until after the Civil War and the surrender of the Apaches that ranching became a major industry.

But the word "cowboy," aside from its usual reference to the person who herded cows on a ranch for a living, can mean many things. As we use the word here, a cowboy is anyone who used a horse for his standard means of travel. That includes practically everyone in the Old West.

The horse provided the fastest means of transportation throughout the West and weren't limited only to "cowboys." Much the same as our technologies develop today, the horse became more important as more people owned them. Oxen, mules, and jackasses were important for hauling freight, but horses provided the speed which was just becoming important.

Today's idea of a "cowboy" has been indelibly created by the movies and television. When people think of cowboys, they picture John Wayne, Clint Eastwood, or someone of that type, whether his occupation was owning a business, herding cattle, being a sheriff, a gunslinger, or just an everyday rancher.

If you saw Clint Eastwood's *The Unforgiven*, you might remember the beginning. He's a widower with two children, who look to be somewhere between six and ten. They live a hardscrabble existence trying to farm and raise pigs. Because there's little official law, he takes an offer to kill a rapist and murderer for money. As he leaves, he tells his son to ride their mule to the nearest neighbor—two miles off—if there's any trouble. And off he goes. (He does make it back, incidentally, and the kids survive the experience.) That really was the way it was in the pioneer days, a hundred years ago.

The "flavor" of Tucson, if you will, has been distilled by two factors. The heat and the isolation. When you think of it, the majority of people in early Tucson must have been good people, because Tucsonans didn't turn sour or mistrustful of newcomers. Living as close as they did to the difference between dead and alive, an extra hand was always welcome. Tucson's arms, like its mountains, have always been open to new friends.

The uncompromising summer heat serves to winnow year-round residents (voluntary ones, anyway) down to those people who know what's important in life. A rattler may stay hidden in the shade under a creosote bush and decline the opportunity of a choice ankle, knowing striking into the noon sun just ain't worth it. Conversely, if a Tucsonan takes the trouble to stand up on his/her hind legs and spout, he or she generally receives the courtesy of a hearing (at least the first few times). Of course, if he proves to be wasting time, Tucsonans aren't shy about saying so, either.

This mix of "live and let live" with "don't tread on me" attracts an outstanding mix of people to Tucson. From comet-hunter David Levy to Linda Ronstadt, world-renowned singer and unabashed celebrant of her Hispanic roots, Tucson has both launched and welcomed some truly unique individuals.

When you travel around the Tucson area, it is hard to realize that the vast distances automobiles so speedily zip through today were once traveled on horseback, mule, or on foot. People now talk about going to San Francisco or San

Diego, knowing that the trip takes a day or so by automobile, or an hour or so by air. In the 1890s people traveled those same distances by horse with practically the same attitude people do today. Instead of "it's only an hour or so away," frontier people said "It's only a week or so away."

There's a story about a man who had been shot in the arm during a gunfight in Tombstone. It took him two days to go the seventy-five miles to Tucson to have a doctor look at it. The doctor did what he could and told the man he'd have to go to San Francisco to have a real doctor look at it. It took him another week to get there by stagecoach! (The man never totally recovered.)

The horse was the first means for quicker transportation. With transportation of people, you also have transportation of information. The ability to move information instantly from place to place has become the hallmark of our modern society.

Back in the 1860s the West Coast was cut off from the rest of the United States. The long distance you had to cover to get from one place of civilization (the East) to the other (the West) was a problem. To get from one place to the other required either a long wagon-train trek or a boat ride around South America and up the West Coast. Either of these methods took months, was very dangerous, and was also very expensive.

Because these were the options for people to travel, they were the also the options for mail and other communications to travel from coast to coast. The gold strikes in California in 1849 and other industries created wealth on the West Coast. Wealth without the means to be recognized or spent will find a way to do so.

As businesses, government, and wealth developed on the West Coast and centered in cities like San Francisco and Los Angeles, the need for speedy communication between the separated business centers grew more and more important. Whereas before it didn't make much difference how long it took news to go from place to place, the business community wanted its information sooner and sooner.

Real Life in the Old West

The Butterfield Overland Trail was one of the elements that was opening up the West to the rest of the United States. Tucson was essential for this route because it provided the only fortified town along the 2,800 miles of trail. It not only afforded protection from robbers and Indians, it was a central place to get provisions and supplies. It became the essential hub and link between the two areas.

Perhaps the best way to get a flavor for the "cowboy and Indian" times in the Southwest is to relate some stories from the latter half of the last century centered around this route, and consequently around Tucson.

In 1857 a businessman from New York, John Butterfield, obtained a government contract to carry mail from St. Louis to San Francisco in twenty-five days. The trail Butterfield followed went south from St. Louis through Indian country to El Paso, Texas. It then led west across the New Mexico Territory to the Colorado River up to Los Angeles and then to San Francisco. They didn't blaze a new trail but followed the so-called "emigrant trail." The Gadsen Purchase had occurred only four years earlier, and Arizona was still part of the New Mexico Territory.

Mules were purchased to pull the coaches. Stations were established about every twenty to twenty-eight miles along the trail, twenty-six of which were in Arizona. The station locations were determined by the availability of water. Tucson is about 130 miles from Apache Pass, the home of the Chiricahua Apaches.

When the Butterfield route first opened, the Apache chief Cochise was friendly with the Americans. His primary enemies were the Mexicans. Butterfield's men entered into agreements with him for safe passage. All went well until 1860.

A troop of about fifty-five soldiers was on the trail trying to find a kidnaped young boy. Although the Apaches were still at peace with the Americans, it was rumored that Cochise had done the deed. Lieutenant Bascom, who was in charge of the troop, invited Cochise and some of his family members to his camp.

Bascom invited Cochise into his tent in the pretext of holding discussions but actually intended to capture him. As soon as Cochise went inside, the tent was surrounded by soldiers. Cochise quickly caught onto the trap. He pulled out a hunting knife concealed in his breech cloth and slashed his way out of the tent. He boldly fought through the line of soldiers and made it to safety.

The family members who accompanied Cochise included his wife, son, half-brother, and two nephews. They were not as lucky. Cochise escaped, but his family was taken hostage. They were later sent to another reservation in the East. Some accounts don't mention his wife, and others say that the people who accompanied Cochise were later hanged.

Cochise quickly rounded up his braves and sent them on the warpath. He attacked the soldiers, wagon trains, and freight wagons moving with the troops. Soldiers were killed; a stage driver who happened along was captured and tortured. He was dragged to death behind Cochise's horse. Eight Mexicans who also happened to be in the area were captured, tied to wagon wheels, tortured, and burned to death. Cochise was not a nice guy when you made him mad.

Bascom knew he was in trouble and went for help. By the time the soldiers returned with help (from Fort Buchanan), they found dead bodies but no Indians. They looked for the Indians for ten days. They either couldn't find them, or wisely wouldn't follow them into their strongholds and gave up the chase.

Cochise's friendly dealings with the Americans had come to an end, and everyone was fair game to him. The Apaches were back on the warpath, and this time the Americans were included as his enemies.

When the Civil War began a year later, the soldiers were pulled back East to fight. Cochise thought he had won his war, and his attacks and raids became even more vicious in an attempt to regain the lands they had lost over the years. In the soldiers' absence there was little protection from the raiding Indians.

When the Union's California Column arrived at Tucson after defeating the small troop of Confederates at Picacho Peak in 1862, they were ordered to continue east to secure the territory. The Indians attacked their scouting parties, hunting parties, and detachments so they knew they were riding into trouble. By the time the scouting detachment got to the well at Apache Pass, Cochise was laying in ambush and attacked. The soldiers were outnumbered and would have been in bad shape had they not fortunately brought cannon and shells with them. These blasted away the hiding places of the Indians and then the Indians themselves.

The soldiers were still surrounded by 600 or so Indians, and the main supply wagons that were following were also in jeopardy. Couriers were sent to warn the supply brigade. They had an ongoing, running fight with a band of Indians led by Mangas Coloradas, supposedly named because he would dip his arms in his victims' blood until red to the shoulders. During the battle he was wounded and the Indians turned back. The couriers got through, saving the supply brigade and supplies.

The battle at Apache Pass went on for two days. The Indians would regain their positions and the fighting continued. Then the cannons blasted away again, killing more Indians. When the Indians realized they couldn't overcome the fire-power of the howitzers, they retreated. The soldiers chose not to follow the Indians into their hideouts in the Chiricahuas. (Mangas' life ended in agony after his capture in 1863. He was tortured and finally decapitated. This last was because the Apache believed mutilation of the body doomed the spirit to wander forever without rest. His skull was eventually sent to the Smithsonian Institution where his brain capacity was adjudged as larger than that of Daniel Webster.)

The Union soldiers weren't the only ones to fall prey to the Apaches. Those Confederate soldiers who on orders decamped from Tucson rather than face the superior numbers of the California Column were also attacked. Four soldiers were killed and thirty-five mules and twenty horses were run off by the Indians.

Tucson's history is replete with stories about the Apaches. For example, the Cienega Springs station, about twenty-five miles east of Tucson, was attacked many times, burned down, and rebuilt. In 1867 W.A. Smith and three companions were attacked there. During the fight that followed, all of Smith's companions were killed by the Apaches. Smith himself shotgunned eight of the Indians and lived to tell the tale. He was known as Shotgun Smith after that.

At Picacho Peak in 1885 a party of twelve people were attacked by thirty to forty Apaches. The fight lasted several hours and ended when other travelers arrived for reinforcements.

Blue Water was another of the stations north of Tucson on the Overland Trail. It was established in 1859 when a well 175 feet deep was dug. This was the only source of water until the Gila River and was a very important station. Because it provided water it was a frequent target of raiding Apaches. Even after the Butterfield Overland Route was closed down because of the Civil War, the well was so important that two soldiers were stationed there full time. In addition to small arms and rifles, they were armed with a cannon.

The station and corrals had been built about 400-500 feet from the well. Raiding Indians made it a habit to water at the well during the night if there were no encampments about. At night the soldiers and the Mexican family that had been hired to maintain the stock locked themselves up behind the thick adobe walls of the station house for protection. Apaches on the raid were always considered dangerous.

Not all Southwestern pioneers lived to tell what happened to them. John W. Baker had accumulated a stake while serving as a wagon master for a Tucson freight company. He brought his wife and small son from Illinois and leased the Blue Water Station where he operated a small store in addition to providing accommodations to travelers. After having a second child, they decided to get out of the hostel business and sold the store.

Baker mentioned to some Mexicans who were working for them that they were going to buy a farm with the money they had gotten from the sale of their business. When Baker was paying them for work they had done, one of them shot him. His wife heard the shot and came to see what happened, carrying her baby. She and the baby were killed by a shotgun blast. Their four-year-old son was shot in the back while running away. The house was ransacked and the murderers took what they could, including two horses and the money, and fled to Mexico. They were never seen again.

People had to respond to situations as they occurred. There usually wasn't enough time to discuss the matter. A man named Charley Harrison was traveling with his friend Fred Anderson from Tucson to Montezuma. When they arrived at Blue Water they found the station keeper and the Mexican family who lived there had been killed by Apaches. The bodies had been scalped but were still warm, so they knew the Indians couldn't be far off.

Anderson went to find some help and within two hours was back with twenty armed men. The posse found the Indians within an hour while they were making camp and after a sharp fight killed them all.

Because the Civil War had taken the soldiers out of the area, the only place that was safe from the Indians was

Tucson. Miners, ranchers, settlers, anyone outside of the Old Pueblo was fair game, not only for attack but probably mutilation and torture as well. It was not a pretty scene. So Tucson filled up with any and all of the people who lived in the region. This meant everyone, regardless of background, education, morals, etc.

In 1863 Arizona was declared a separate territory from New Mexico. Charles D. Poston, later known as the father of Arizona, was appointed Superintendent of Indian Affairs for Arizona. He was in San Francisco at the time and arranged for transportation and a military escort to Arizona. A newspaper reporter by the name of Brown, the Don Rickles of his day and an old friend of Poston's, decided to make the trip with him and report on things as they went along the way. Poston was traveling throughout the entire state and eventually made it to Tucson—at that time the only town in the Territory. The reporter didn't seem to think too highly of it:

> Tucson is the most wonderful scatteration of human habituations the mind has ever beheld. It is a city of mud boxes, dingy and dilapidated, cracked and baked into a composite of dust and filth littered about with broken corrals, sheds, bake-ovens, carcasses of dead animals, and broken pottery; barren of verdure, parched, naked, and grimly desolate in the glare of the southern sun. Adobe walls without whitewash inside or out, hard earth-floors, baked and dried Mexicans, sorebacked burrows, coyote dogs, and terra-cotta children; soldiers, teamsters and honest miners lounging about the mescal shops, soaked with fiery poison; a noise band of Sonoran buffoons, dressed in theatrical posture, cutting their antics in the public places to the most diabolical din of fiddles and guitars ever heard; a long train of government wagons preparing to start for Fort Yuma or the Rio Grande—these are the things the traveler

sees, and a great many things more, but in vain he looks for a hotel or lodging-house.

The Poston party didn't stay long in Tucson, only long enough to get provisions. Because the Apaches were in full control of the area, a company of thirty soldiers from Tucson was assigned to escort Poston's party. As a parting shot, Browne wrote, "I must be permitted to say that the best view of Tucson is the rear view on the road to Fort Yuma."

In 1864 Tucson became an incorporated town. One of its most popular citizens, William Oury, a former Texas Ranger was appointed mayor. Oury was responsible for one of the blackest days in Tucson's history. In 1871 he and a number of prominent Tucson citizens organized and led a band of vigilantes on a raid of an Apache camp near Camp Grant on the San Pedro River northeast of Tucson. It was supposedly a camp of hostile Indians.

All the men and warriors had left the camp, however. The vigilantes killed seventy-seven women and eight old men. The Camp Grant Massacre resulted in condemning headlines and the outrage of politicians and citizens across the country. The posse was finally brought to trial, but Oury and the others were acquitted. Western justice at the time might best be illustrated by a comment made by the wife of one of the raiders, a well-known businessman. She stated that while her husband wasn't proud of the role he had taken, the Indians were so dangerous that "it had to be done."

Without making any judgement, the desert was a difficult place to live, for anyone.

Survival of early Tucsonans was sometimes a matter of sheer stubbornness. One day a fellow named Rhodes returned to his ranch just south of Tucson to find that all of his family and ranch hands had been killed by Indians. Because the Indians were still in the area, he himself was in a dangerous situation. He managed to avoid most of them, but a small group discovered him and chased him until his horse gave out. He made it to a stand of willows and holed up there to fight for his life. He was wounded in the elbow and propped it up in the sand to stop the bleeding.

As the story goes, he was down to his last two bullets when the Indians rushed him in a final attack. He managed to shoot the one in the lead, which stopped the attack and caused them to back off. After some discussion among themselves, the Indians demanded that he surrender. No fool, Rhodes told them where they could put it. They discussed the matter a bit more and eventually rode off, leaving him alone because he put up such a brave fight. There was one bullet left in his gun.

Following the treachery of Lt. Bascom, Cochise declared war in 1862. It wasn't until 1872 that peace was made. During this time, a rancher by the name of Tom Jeffords had made friends with Cochise by bravely walking into his camp, alone and unarmed, asking for peace with the Indians for him and his family. The story goes that Cochise was so impressed by this courageous act that he and Jeffords became blood brothers in a tribal ceremony. (This story was popularized twice, first by the 1950 Jeff Chandler movie and later in the television series originally televised in the mid-1950s, both entitled *Broken Arrow*.)

It was through Jeffords' help that peace was made. But the white men still weren't happy. The Indians still lived on lands that they wanted. They continued to harass the Indians and broke the treaty in many ways. The Chiricahua Apaches kept their side of the treaty until 1876 when Cochise died. His son Taza tried to maintain the power his father had but slowly lost it.

Once more the Indians went on the warpath against both Americans and Mexicans. Apache chiefs such as Geronimo, Juh, Natchex, and Loco are some of the more famous names that have come down to us.

In 1886 Colonel Stone, for whom Stone Avenue in Tucson is named, was operating a gold mine. He started out for Tucson with a gold shipment from his mine in a chartered stage. Accompanying Stone were the driver, a shotgun guard, and four troopers protecting the coach. The group noticed that a group of Indians were trailing them. Somewhere along they way they decided to bury the gold and make a run for it before the Indians could catch up with them. They buried the gold but never made it. They were all captured and tortured to death. No one ever found the gold.

Chato was an Apache who played a significant role in the surrender of the Apaches. He had been one of the fiercest and pitiless Apache chiefs during the 1870s. In 1883 Chato made a pledge with General Crook, who had ridden into Mexico on an expedition against him. Chato agreed to remain at peace with the United States government. He returned to the reservation where he had the best farm, and also enlisted in the army. Chato, a sergeant, commanded a company of Apache scouts. More than scouts, they were responsible for tracking Geronimo and his band of cohorts down and convincing them to surrender in 1886.

The Chiricahua Apaches who surrendered with Geronimo were treated badly. They were moved to Florida where, because of poor living conditions, many died. They were then moved to Alabama in a half-hearted attempt to correct the situation, but many more died. They were eventually settled on a reservation in Oklahoma.

Now the road to Tucson was comparatively safe from Indians, but there were other dangers to take their place. Murder and mayhem were everywhere. Lawlessness was often dealt with outside of the courts, and such instances were often as not reported quite matter-of-factly in the *Tucson Citizen*.

For instance in Adamsville, a settlement north of Tucson, a man by the name of John Willis was accused of shooting an unarmed man for no apparent reason. It was an open and shut case, but for some reason Willis wasn't arrested. Taking advantage of the situation, he made his way out of Adamsville down to Tucson. Arriving a couple of days later, he was arrested and tried for the murder. He was found guilty and sentenced to hang.

While he was in the Tucson jail waiting for an appeal to the Supreme Court, other things that would seal his fate were happening. One night a prominent Tucson store keeper and his wife were murdered in their beds. They were gruesome murders, and a search was immediately started for the culprits, three men who were in the area the day before.

There was no question they were guilty. When they were captured they still had goods stolen from the bodies and the store on them. They were placed in the jail with Willis.

The following day, after the couple was buried, the angry townspeople gathered in front of the jail. They erected two large posts about twelve feet apart. Across the top of them and running between them they placed another post. A couple of wagons waited underneath. Four nooses were thrown over the pole.

The four prisoners were dragged from the jail with black bags over their heads. The murderers were put on the wagons and nooses placed around their necks. Then the horses were whipped and justice done.

The *Tucson Citizen* (which remains a major newspaper in the Tucson area) reported that an inquest in the matter was made. The jury stated that the hangings were done by the people of Tucson *en masse* and that in view of the murders that had been committed by the three and the tardiness of the justice regarding John Willis, a murderer, that the extreme measures taken by the citizens of Tucson was in vindication of their lives, their property, and the peace and good order of society. It was regretted that such actions had to take place, but in light of the fact that criminals were allowed to go unpunished they had little other choice. That was the end of the matter.

The stage line north of Tucson led to California. In 1876 it took five days and nights to go from Tucson to San Diego and cost ninety dollars "hard" money. At the time, dollars were worth only a small percentage of their face value, and almost everything was paid for in gold or silver.

The rate schedule in May 1876 was Tucson to Florence $8, to Maricopa Wells $18, to Phoenix $20, to Wickenburg $40, to Prescott $40, to Yuma $40, to San Diego $50. The total "dollars" for this trip amount to $216, versus the $90 hard money mentioned above.

Meals at the stage stations cost a dollar. The coaches traveled about five miles per hour. That was schedule time. It took three days and nights just to go from Yuma to San Diego. Because the stations never knew exactly when the stage would be coming through, each stop took about an hour. The horses had to be changed, food prepared for about eight people, wagons wheels greased, and other necessities attended to. None of this was started until the stage had actually arrived at the station.

In March 1882 in Tombstone, Morgan Earp challenged Bob Hatch to a pool game. While they were playing, a shot was fired through the back door and Morgan Earp was killed. They found where someone had stood on a box and fired the shot through the upper half of the door, which was made out of glass. The Earps suspected a certain Frank Stillwell of committing the murder.

When they took their brother's body to Tucson seventy-five miles away, Stillwell saw the Earps on the train coming into town. Stillwell went around the rear of the train, supposedly with the intention of shooting more of the Earps. Gunshots were heard. The next morning Stillwell's body was found riddled with bullets. It appears the Earps had their revenge for the murder of their brother.

As with all things, time brought changes to Tucson. As "civilization" came to the West, law and order took control. The people who had come to Tucson to live a decent life found that their influence was taking hold.

In 1896 Tucson was the port of entry from Mexico. It was now reported to be a rather nice town. The few (white) families living there were great hosts. Fort Lowell, about eight miles east on the Rillito Creek, was also a lively place, and the officers and their wives vied with the good people in Tucson in entertaining.

The Mexican influence on Tucson was more than just political. Until 1854 Tucson was a part of Northern Mexico. The customs, clothing, living habits, the entire culture was that of a Mexican town in Apache country. Trade was done primarily through the Mexican port of Guaymas.

The first successful businessmen in Tucson, freight haulers, were of Mexican descent. Because most of the Anglos who later moved to Tucson were single males, intermarriage between them and the established families was inevitable. Sam Hughes and Hiram S. Stevens, two of the most prominent men in Tucson's business history married sisters, Atanacia and Petra Santa Cruz.

In 1880 the long awaited rail line was completed. Since the 1840s there had been considerable talk about a transcontinental railroad, but it was only after the Civil War that things began to happen. The railroads were a chancy investment. Many went out of business before they were able to complete laying their track.

The Southern Pacific Railroad was successful. They began building from San Francisco and worked their way to San Diego and East from there. On March 20, 1880, the Southern Pacific celebrated the completion of the line to Tucson. The railroad came to Tucson for a number of reasons, among them the discovery of the silver mines in Tombstone. The line ultimately ran to El Paso.

With the coming of the railroad, freight lines eventually went out of business. The entrepreneurs who owned them didn't wait long to establish other businesses. Others went into ranching or mining.

In the 1880s many families came from Sonora, Mexico to Tucson. Until the 1930s they constituted an ethnic and political majority. Names familiar in Tucson history are Leopold Carillo, Sabino Otero, Carlos Jacome, and Frederick Ronstadt (grandfather of Linda Ronstadt).

Mexicans also took part in the political scene of Tucson. Prior to becoming a state in 1912, Francisco Solano Leon, Juan Elias and his brother Jesus Maria Elias, and Mariano Samaniego served in the Territorial Legislature. One of our earliest mayors was Estevan Ochoa.

Tucson's Native American Heritage

Tucson's culture also has a component from our Native American residents. Many Indians have lived in the Tucson area, some say for as long as 35,000 years. While their civilizations have waxed and waned over the centuries, the remaining peoples carried forward the cultures, languages, and practices.

The Sobaipure, Papago, or Pima Indians occupied the land when Fr. Kino arrived in the 1690s. For the most part they were a peaceful people. They were bitter enemies of the Apaches who lived to the east and frequently raided the Papago camps. The Papagos welcomed the protection they received from the Spanish army.

The Tohono O'odham Nation

The Pimas were known as Papagos until 1986 when the Papago Tribe of Arizona approved a new constitution. They changed their name to the Tohono O'odham Nation (simply, the Desert People), to differentiate themselves from other Pima Indians living further north around Phoenix.

The Tohono O'odham Reservation contains 2.7 million acres of land, roughly the size of Northern Ireland and second in size only to the Navajo Reservation. It is comprised of three separate sites, the San Xavier Reservation (south of Tucson), the Gila Bend Reservation, and the Sells Reservation, some distance to the southwest.

Another group of Native Americans who live in the Tucson area are the Yaqui. Their name in Yaqui is "Yoeme." Yaquis have lived here since the early part of the eighteenth century. In 1910, after the Mexican revolution, a large number of Yaquis moved from their homeland along the Rio Yaqui in southern Sonora, Mexico to the Tucson area. In 1978 the Yaquis organized as the Pascua Yaqui Association and achieved recognition. The northern border of the mile square Pascua Yaqui Indian Reservation runs along the south side of Valencia road, west of I-19. They have 200 acres of separated reservation in and around the city.

Reservation lands are held in Federal Trust, and are thereby exempt from state and local property taxes. State, county, and other local laws do not apply on Indian reservations to enrolled members of the tribes unless federal law prescribes otherwise. Federal law takes precedence over tribal ordinances. (Evidence of this was seen in 1994 when the FBI confiscated numerous slot machines from the Tohono O'odhams over a dispute about gambling.)

Speaking about gambling, there are two "Las Vegas" style casinos built on the reservations. Desert Diamond Casino on the Tohono O'odham's San Xavier Reservation was the first. The Pascua Yaquis operate the Casino of the Sun on theirs. Gaming enthusiasts can play slot machines or choose between video poker, keno, blackjack, and craps machines. Bingo enthusiasts won't be disappointed at either casino. These business ventures have created a source of income for many Native Americans, and through distribution of profits, provide new schools and social centers that otherwise would not have been available.

Moving to the other end of the spectrum, the San Xavier Reservation is also home to the San Xavier Mission. It was founded in 1700 at the site of what was then a Papago village by the Jesuit missionary Father Eusebio Francisco Kino. The first church built on the site was destroyed during the Pima Revolt of 1751, and in 1767 the Spanish crown forced the Jesuits out of the New World. The Franciscans began construction in 1783 of what would become the beautiful "White Dove of the Desert." It is still in use today, a parish church.

San Xavier Mission, the White Dove of the Desert, is on the Tohono O'odham Indian Reservation (Photo courtesy of Kevilee Schaich)

Reservation Manners

Remember, whether looking for the cat and the mouse on San Xavier's facade or watching the Easter Yaqui celebration, visitors to reservation lands are invited guests. This is an invitation that can be revoked at any time. Reservations aren't museums; they're where people live. Here's how to have a pleasant experience while leaving a good feeling behind you.

Respect your host's customs. Modest dress is recommended, particularly if you visit traditional villages. Remember not all Indians tribes are alike. Each has its unique culture, traditions, and customs.

Don't trespass. Don't go barging up to people's homes or traipsing through their yards. Ask permission before going into places that aren't clearly open to the public. Most importantly, if you notice pottery shards or other archeological artifacts, leave them alone. Ignoring for the moment the potential penalties, both federal, state and tribal, leaving archeological finds in situ for the professionals also serves to add to our knowledge of people long vanished from here.

Learn a little. Tohono O'odham is not an Irish name. It means "Desert People," and is pronounced "Toe-HO-no AH-tomb." The Tohono O'odham officially dropped the name "Papago" in 1986. To refer to the tribe using only one name, use O'odham, the "people."

Both of the tribes in the Tucson area use the term chairman for their tribal leaders, not "chief."

Both the O'odham and Yaqui speak Spanish as their primary language, but English is a common second language among them.

Make sure you're legal. If you've come to the reservation to fish or hunt, you have to have tribal permits (not state licenses). This may also pertain to activities such as boating and backpacking. Call tribal tourism offices, game and fish departments, or police in advance of your trip. Checking out and conforming to their requirements is your responsibility.

Listen. If you ask a question, listen to the answer. Especially if an elder is speaking, give them your full attention.

Don't take it for granted that photographs are okay. Check ahead about photographic, video, or audio taping restrictions. While tribal ceremonies and rituals may be open to public view, some may ban not only photographs but sketches. Remember that this isn't a museum or something put on for show, but are intimate parts of people's lives and beliefs. Consider your reaction if your Easter service were interrupted by lights and cameras.

This goes double when photographing individuals. Ask first, and if you're ignored or a fee is requested, don't take it personally.

The makeup and face of Tucson's personality have changed throughout the years. Starting as a place along the river that provided water and a good place to live, it developed into a way-station and place of protection from the war-like people who lived around it, and has become a city whose populations have come from three different countries.

You see this background in the faces of the people of the city. Anglos, Mexican, Indians—people from all races. The cowboy, Indian, and "pioneer" influence cannot be missed. Dress is rarely formal. The dress code for smaller businesses is practically nonexistent. As long as you are dressed neatly in clean and untorn clothes and have good hygiene, you are set to do business in Tucson. Dress-down days at the local "formal" businesses, such as banks and branch offices of nation-wide companies, feature jeans, cowboy boots, and ten-gallon hats.

There is one eating establishment, a cowboy restaurant named Pinnacle Peak, on the east side of town on Tanque Verde Road in the Trail Dust Town shopping center, that boasts of its reputation for forbidding ties on the premises. A warning on the door announces that ties are not permitted. Inside, the ceilings are decorated with the truncated remnants of the ties of unwary guests who did not believe the warning.

Dress Western

Not everyone gets carried away with the Western look, happily. In fact, the people walking down Tucson streets look much like any other crowd on any urban street. Well, maybe not exactly like. At least partially because of the climate here, in both manners and dress Tucson tends to be casual. Even though today's offices and businesses are air conditioned, more formal business wear as it's known in the East and Mid-West is the exception, not the rule.

In February, however, when the Rodeo comes to town—that's when "dressing Western" comes into its own. Here's a short rundown of some of the sartorial potential this can entail.

Stetson

Starting at the top, the hat. Stetson is the best-known name when it comes to cowboy hats. Originally these shaped-felt chapeaus were everything from the only roof a cowboy had, to his cup at the watering hole (his and his horse's). Today they still help keep the sun off, but I'll pass on the drink.

Kerchief

The kerchief around the cowboy's neck was also a multipurpose item, from wiping off sweat to filtering dust from a herd of cows. Unfortunately, use of the original blue/black/white and red/black/white patterns have been more or less preempted by gang members. (We told you Tucson was a modern city! Didn't you listen?) Nowadays kerchief wearers are more likely to choose silk, and in a stunning shade.

Bolo Tie

An acceptable Western alternative to the kerchief (without returning to the much-shunned necktie) is the bolo tie. This is a length of braided leather that is looped around the wearer's neck, with the two ends (which are usually tipped with metal) dangling down in front. The loose ends are kept from utter anarchy by a sliding clasp, and here's where people get really creative. We've seen bolo tie clasps with everything from gem-quality turquoise to (shudder) Lucite-encased scorpions.

Incidentally, "acceptable alternative" is just what it sounds like. Some of the state's most important people have been seen at quite formal events in bolo ties.

Jeans

Of course, the most basic item of a cowboy outfit is a pair of jeans. Levi Strauss made his fortune selling pants made of sailcloth to sourdoughs in the Gold Rush. The rugged combination of riveted seams and durable cloth continue to make jeans a favorite part of nearly everyone's wardrobe.

Belts

Of course, if you're going to wear cowboy pants, you have to wear a cowboy belt to hold them up. Evidence of a cowboy belt is a large, preferably silver belt buckle. The bigger the better.

Squaw Dresses

There's also a feminine side to Western wear. Currently a fashion seen almost exclusively at rodeo time or at square dance exhibitions, "squaw dresses" were actually invented here in Tucson. Also called the "broomstick dress," these elaborately decorated, full-skirted creations were a national fashion in the 1950s. They retained their popularity in their home town, however, and today are seeing renewed interest from square-dance enthusiasts.

The outfit consists of a three-tired skirt worn with a matching top, always in a solid color, no prints. The style of the blouse varies, from elasticized off-the-shoulder puffs to long sleeves with a collar. The skirt, gathered at each tier, is tightly pleated. Originally, this was done by wrapping it around a broomstick, thus its second name. Wider than full circle, the dress's defining feature is its ornamentation. At least the lower two tiers of the skirt are edged in row after row of braid and ric-rac, matching and contrasting the color of the skirt. The ornamentation of the blouse depends on its style, but it's the skirt that distinguishes this style of dress.

Cowboy Boots

Boots seem to have played a big part in a cowboy's life. "He died with his boots on." "Boot Hill." "He couldn't pour spit out of a boot if the instructions were written on the heel." Completely utilitarian, there's reasons why boots are made the way they are. The higher heel provides a rider with something substantial to catch on the stirrup. This is important when it makes the difference between staying on or losing your transportation. The height of the boot on the leg serves to protect riders' legs from brush, as well as serve as a deterrent to anything attacking at ankle-height (like a rattler).

Guest Ranches and Resorts

Once known as "dude" ranches, guest ranches were originally working cattle ranches where the owner wanted a little additional income during the winter. As visitors learned how enjoyable the mix of our mild winters with a taste of the "Old West" was, their popularity grew.

If you want a good idea of how cowboys might have lived, spend some time as a guest at one of these ranches. Some were actually working ranches at one time and some still are. Others exist solely to provide their guests with a close-up look at the Sonora Desert.

In keeping with the Old West heritage, depending on how wide you swing the loop, the Tucson area can boast up to eleven guest ranches. There used to be six guest ranches with Tucson addresses. At the time of this writing, however, two (Paz Entera and Wild Horse) are in transition. The other four offer everything from birdwatching to skeet-shooting and hammocks—oh, and of course, horseback riding and hiking. All guest ranches welcome children, and several have programs specifically aimed at the younger set.

While accommodations at the guest ranches discussed above are far from harsh, if your tastes run more to being pampered, Tucson boasts some of the most luxurious resorts in the world. Tucson enjoys more sunshine, about 350 sunny days per year, than any other city in the United States. Winter temperatures are mild and attract visitors who are looking for respite from the cold and snow of the north. This carries on a tradition begun following the First World War, when the Veterans Hospital was built here to serve as a sanitarium for soldiers who would be able to take advantage of the climate and desert air.

The first big resort in Tucson was the El Conquistador, located where El Con Mall now is. Today, only its water tower survives (see page 150). There are dozens of resorts in the Tucson area, offering every amenity you can imagine from world-class golf courses to complete spa facilities. They have become part of the modern southwestern experience. For more information on ranches and resorts see pages 174-177.

Totally Tucson

Tucson has a style all its own; casual, western, and most of all, real. Everyone who chooses to has a right to live here. No one is better than another. What is "politically correct" doesn't hold too much water in the desert. "Being responsible for what you do and say" is what matters.

For instance, if you "surf the Internet" you might run across the Old Pueblo Trolley home page. It typifies the Tucson mentality:

> Catch the trolley on Fourth Avenue between Eighth Street and University Blvd, or on University Boulevard between Fourth Avenue and the west gate of the University of Arizona.

The trolley's summer schedule reads as follows:

Weekdays: No Lunchtime operation (too hot!)
Weekends: Friday: 6 p.m. till 10 p.m. (Maybe later if busy).
          Saturday: 10 a.m. till Midnight.
          Sunday: 12 Noon till 6 p.m.

This casual yet realistic attitude is a hallmark of true Tucsonans: The trolley runs up and down these two streets; if you want a ride, flag it down. Because it's too hot to run at noon in the summer, we don't run.

This chapter brings you in touch with interesting places in Tucson that typify the realistic attitude of its citizens. Tucson, surrounded by miles of empty Sonoran Desert, expects to provide something for everyone, whatever your tastes or preferences. There isn't room to list all the events and activities available in Tucson. Two excellent publications that list most attractions in Tucson are readily available. The *Tucson Official Visitors Guide* is published by the Metropolitan Tucson Convention and Visitors Bureau. Their office is at 130 South Scott Avenue. The other is the *Tucson Guide Quarterly*, published by Madden Publishing, Inc. P.O. Box 42915, Tucson, AZ 85733. Whether you live in Tucson or are visiting, these publications are well worth consulting.

Festivals and Celebrations

A large part of Tucson is wedded to the Mexican and Indian heritages. These heritages are more sanquine and earthy than cold and sophisticated. Festivals and celebrations follow the most basic patterns of the earth. Because these are annual events, it is important to know when in the year they are held.

Spring is a wonderful time in Tucson. Among other reasons, that's when three different Native American festivals are held in the area.

Wa:k Powwow

The Wa:k Powwow is a weekend-long celebration that brings members of over twenty different tribes to the San Xavier Reservation. The Tohono O'odham tribe hosts this assemblage where war and hoop dancers demonstrate their art. Both individuals and groups perform these traditional dances. While the public is welcome, please ask permission before filming or taping anyone, whether performing or not. There is a small admission fee. Native American food favorites such as frybread and chili are sold, as are baskets, rugs, and jewelry.

Waila Festival

The Tohono O'odham Waila (Why-la) Festival is held in the spring at the Arizona Historical Society. Over a hundred years old, waila is a type of music sometimes called "chicken scratch." Waila bands include both six-string and bass guitars, drums, a button accordion, and an alto sax. Waila music is traditionally played during night-long saints day feasts, birthdays, or graduations, often combining music from several popular Mexican songs.

Traditional waila dances are performed during the festival by O'odham elders, passing on the steps to a new generation. Artisans also make the trip to the museum, demonstrating traditional O'odham basketry and pottery techniques. Hungry visitors can sample favorites such as frybread, chili, and tortillas from the food booths.

Palm Fiesta

There are three Yaqui villages in the Tucson area; Pasqua Yaqui Reservation (West Valencia and South Camino de Oeste), Old Pasqua Village (West Grant Road and I-10), and Yaqui Village, also called Barrio Libre (South 39th Street and West 10th Avenue). From the beginning of Lent through Easter, ceremonies that mix tribal traditions with Catholic ritual are held.

❏ While the Yaqui open their ceremonies to visitors, please keep in mind that this is a religious celebration, not a show or act. No audio or visual recording is permitted—not even note-taking. Please respect their wishes.

The Palm Fiesta starts on the eve of Palm Sunday. During Holy Week, participants reenact Easter from the Yaqui perspective with ceremonial dancing. This passion play follows through the crucifixion and resurrection, and is open to the public. It culminates Easter Sunday, with good triumphing over evil once again.

Fiesta de San Agustín

The Arizona Historical Society Museum hosts the Fiesta de San Agustín in late August. The original fiesta began around 1775 as a religious festival to honor St. Augustine, Tucson's patron saint. During the 1800s it evolved into a more secular observation, but its popularity waned as the ethnic mix in Tucson became more Anglo than Hispanic.

In 1983 the society brought the fiesta back as a cultural event. Usually held the last weekend in August, many different performances take place both inside the museum and outside on its grounds. Visitors can enjoy a variety of Mexican and Native American music and dancing, food booths, children's games, and other presentations. The food booths are elaborately decorated, and with reason. Every year a contest judges the ornamentation, and prizes are awarded.

Fiesta de los Vaqueros

The Southwestern experience wouldn't be complete without a rodeo. In February the Fiesta de los Vaqueros comes to Tucson. Tucsonans think it's important enough to close the schools for two days to give kids a chance to celebrate the Cowboy Festival too!

Every year some unsuspecting out-of-state visitor gets a surprise. For the last thirty-six years the Pima County Sheriff's Department and the Tucson Junior Chamber of Commerce have "arrested" a traveling couple to become Tucson's honored Welcome Travelers.

A sheriff's car pulls an unsuspecting automobile with out-of-state license plates over to the side of I-10 somewhere along the downtown area. The occupants are greeted with the unwelcome words "You are under arrest!" Once the couple calms down a bit, they're informed that they will be the guests of the Tucson Rodeo for the duration.

After a photo opportunity at a traveling hoosegow, complete with bars, they're presented with their very own wanted posters and are treated, with the help of local restaurateurs and businesses, to a five-day stay at a local hotel, free meals, official Western outfits, trips to Old Tucson and the Arizona-Sonora Desert Museum, and front row seats for multiple events of the Tucson Rodeo. Of course, the couple doesn't know that when they see the deputy pulling them over, and doesn't always appreciate the fact. In 1992 it took eleven tries before a couple agreed to the honor.

The Fiesta is more than just a rodeo. Tucson welcomes in the rodeo with a unique parade. Residents and visitors join each other lining up along streets to watch the longest (one and one-half miles) and oldest (1996 hosted the 71st Festival) nonmotorized parade in the world. No engines are allowed. Where else can you see saloon gals, modern-day politicians, and rodeo clowns riding side-by-side down the middle of the street? Not an internal combustion engine in the lot—horses, buggies, and stagecoaches share the parade route. There's quite a few of them. In 1996 there were more than 250 entries, including almost 4,000 people, 22 bands, more than 100 wagons and buggies, and about 800 horses.

The easiest way to get to the parade route and back is to take advantage of the Rodeo shuttle. SunTrans (Tucson's bus line) offers a special pass on parade day. They run a number of shuttles, usually from shopping malls, dropping people off near the grandstands at Irvington and Sixth. For the best seats try to get there before 8:00 a.m. The parade always begins at 9:00 a.m. and the shuttles continue to run until after noon. Over 200,000 people lined up along the way in 1996 to view the festivities.

The rodeo itself is one of the last survivors of the real working West, and runs from Thursday afternoon through Sunday. What are now judged events in a performance ring were once everyday chores that the working ranch hand or cowboy performed. Horses had to be broken before they could be ridden. Calves had to be cut out from the herd and branded, so good roping and riding skills were basic necessities.

What began as a cowboy's way of measuring his skills against his peers evolved into a new way of life. Whether on a ranch or in the arena, the same skills stand cowboys of any era in good stead. Instead of following the herd or moving from bunkhouse to bunkhouse, the majority of today's working cowboys are found on the rodeo circuit. Events include everything from bronc and bull riding and bulldogging to team calf roping and barrel racing (a woman's event).

Winterhaven

Christmas in Tucson may not be white (barring a trip to Mt. Lemmon), but don't let anyone tell you the sprit of Christmas is missing from this part of the desert. Tucson has Winterhaven.

This subdivision was created in 1949 by William Otto Fraesdorf Joli Ryan, a cattle ranch broker. He worked with C.B. Richards, owner of the property, to design Winterhaven. Residents of the neighborhood are required by contract to put up holiday decorations at Christmas.

The Winterhaven subdivision is bordered by East Fort Lowell Road, North Country Club Road, East Prince Road, and North Tucson Boulevard. Since its opening, most of its 270 homeowners have delighted in the friendly competition, each choosing a distinctive theme to follow in decorating their houses and yards. Some of the displays are animated, and many are accompanied by appropriate music, and everywhere you look is the glitter of thousands of lights.

The subdivision opens for visitors in mid-December and runs for two weeks. It always attracts many visitors—so many that traffic is controlled by setting aside certain nights for walking tours only. Other nights, visitors can still beat the crush by taking advantage of the special shuttles Sun-Trans runs through the area. While the fare isn't high ($1 or so), if you bring two cans of food for the Community Food Bank, you can ride free. If you prefer Christmas with a rustic flavor, several companies offer the option of riding through the subdivision on a hay wagon or in a horse-drawn carriage.

Tucson Meet Yourself

Tucson Meet Yourself is a wonderful celebration, and everyone in Tucson is invited! It was started in 1974 by Jim Griffith. He's a folklorist and the Director of the University of Arizona's Southwest Folklore Center. Tucson Meet Yourself is held in October and is a painless way to introduce yourself to the incredible cultural variety of people who live in Tucson.

This multicultural conglomeration of crafts booths, ethnic demonstrations, and food choices demonstrates as nothing else can the strength of Tucson's diversity. The continuous entertainment may jump from Western square dancing to Yiddish folk dancing to the sound of bagpipes from Tucson's own pipers. Choose a blintz from one booth, an eggroll from another, have a piece of frybread with honey, and wash it down with stout. This festival offers children's entertainment as well, and runs three days (okay, three evenings and two days) so you have no excuse not to take advantage of it.

Downtown Saturday Night

Quite similar to Tucson Meet Yourself, Downtown Saturday Night is a twice-monthly affair. The first Saturday of the month has an artistic flavor. It focuses on the arts district, and the studios and galleries put their best foot forward and invite the public inside.

The third Saturday of the month is the second Downtown Saturday Night, and this one concentrates on bringing the public back to downtown merchants. Stores and shops stay open between 7:00 and 10:00 p.m., with music from street musicians enticing jugglers and dancers out into the open.

During both nights the Tucson Public Market is also open. Locally grown fruits, vegetables, and grains are available (in season, of course) as well as a fine assortment of arts and crafts from local artisans.

Places to See

The Arizona-Sonora Desert Museum

If you have time to visit only one place in Tucson, the consensus among visitors and residents alike is to visit the Arizona-Sonora Desert Museum.

Why? Because the museum is more a zoo than a museum. In this one place you can see almost every type of plant and animal that lives in this area, alive, and in their native habitat. In fact, you could live in Tucson your entire life, and still see something new at the museum.

Here you see the desert few people see, unless they spend most of their life outside. Both living (mountain lion to rattlesnake) and nonliving (geology) exhibits allow you to experience the complete range of life in the desert. Hawks and turkey buzzards are seen close up during presentations given by museum staff. The birds used for these presentations are those injured and unable to safely return to the wild. Their participation in these presentations helps museum visitors to understand the interdependence of all desert life.

Explore a desert riparian habitat, and enjoy the under-water antics of the otters. Learn about the dynamics of a prairie dog town. Observe Mexican wolves and black bears in their natural setting. There's even a limestone cave to walk through, and the adjoining earth history room takes you through the geological history of our earth, including a rock from the moon.

If reptiles and invertebrates are your cup of tea, just off the entrance is an exhibit specializing in these. A useful place to visit, since it's always nice to know if the snake that's crossing your path is a rattler or not. And don't forget the fish and amphibian exhibit across the way.

Perhaps the most popular attraction since it opened is the hummingbird aviary. Walk inside this enclosure, sit down, and enjoy. Hummingbirds of all varieties live inside. If you wear a Hawaiian print, you may even have an up-close encounter with one!

Old Tucson

Old Tucson has been the site and movie location for many Westerns. A popular attraction, it has become quite famous. But on April 24, 1995, Tucson residents turned on their television sets and watched in horror as TV news crews reported the destruction of Old Tucson.

Around seven in the evening a blaze of unknown origin swept through the fifty-six-year-old movie studio and park. (While arson is seriously suspected, at this writing there is no confirmation.) As night fell, watchers at Gate's Pass could see nothing but scarlet flames eating their way through this monument to the West. Over 200 emergency personnel fought the blaze, while park patrons, employees, and animals fled. The next day, the *Arizona Daily Star*'s headline read "Blaze destroys Old Tucson; Landmark is engulfed in minutes."

Happily, the obituary for Old Tucson proved to be partly premature. When the embers cooled and an assessment could be made, it was discovered that less than half of the structures in the seventy-acre park had sustained damage, but it was enough to close the attraction.

Nothing but ashes remained in the Mexican Plaza, through Front and Kansas streets, White Oaks, and the Lincoln County Court House. Even the sound stage had burned. But down on the south end of the town, some of the original set from *Arizona* still stood.

After the fire, visitors, well-wishers, and callers convinced Old Tucson's operators that the center was still a popular destination. Almost immediately, the process of rebuilding began, and it is anticipated that the park will reopen by the end of December 1996.

While Front Street will undoubtedly rise again, not everything can be rebuilt or restored. Nothing but ashes remain of sets and props from epics filmed here. Costumes from *Little House on the Prairie*, *High Chaparral*, and *Rio Bravo*, are among those lost.

While Old Tucson itself is closed and rebuilding, The Last Outpost retail store is open for visitors to keep track of the progress. Here you can find souvenirs of the park, including some ash from the fire, as well as videos of Old Tucson as it was prior to the disaster. The Last Outpost is currently open from 10:00 a.m. to 5:00 p.m.

Old Tucson has provided a backdrop to many films and television productions. It was the summer of 1939 when Columbia Pictures decided to make the movie *Arizona*. The moviemakers decided to use a patch of land on the western face of the Tucson Mountains. Before beginning construction of the sets they first did their homework.

Using street maps and photographs of Tucson as it had appeared in the 1860s, a reproduction of Old Tucson quickly grew under the desert sun.

Arizona, with William Holden and Jean Arthur in the lead roles, premiered in 1940 at Tucson's Temple of Music and Art (and four other downtown Tucson theaters). It was quite the social occasion. As part of the celebration, busloads of visitors drove down the dusty dirt road of Gate's Pass to become the first visitors of what was to become Old Tucson.

Over the years Old Tucson has experienced its ups and downs. World War II intervened, however, and in 1942 Pima County bought up both the film set and an additional 3,200 acres of adjoining federal land for $1.25 an acre. After the war, the Tucson Jaycees signed a five-year, $1-a-year lease with the county for the town. They began refurbishing the place, and in the fall of 1947 they held a fiesta welcoming all of Tucson.

With the Jaycee's using the yearly fiestas to finance the refurbishment, Old Tucson grew in size and popularity. Soon Hollywood rediscovered the place. Then in the 1950s Robert Shelton blew into town. He signed a new ten-year lease with Pima County in 1959. After a $400,000 facelift, Old Tucson reopened in late January 1960 to record crowds and has been a landmark for the city ever since.

As the popularity of Western movies waxed and waned, so did the popularity of Old Tucson. As long as "riding into the sunset" and "head 'em off at the pass" are part of the American vocabulary, Old Tucson will have a place in our hearts.

San Xavier Mission

The name of the designer of the White Dove of the Desert is unknown, as is the reason for the incomplete tower. The mission, south of Tucson on the Tohono O'odham Reservation, was completed in 1797 by Jesuit missionaries, only for the Jesuits themselves to be expelled in 1828. Shortly after, the mission was closed. It was returned to service as a church in 1913, the year after Arizona became a state, and Mass is held there daily.

San Xavier is one of the most elaborately decorated of the Jesuit missions, beginning with the facade which is covered with carvings. Of particular interest are a cat and a mouse perched on the swirls atop the two outside pillars. On one perches a crouching cat, on the other a mouse. The local legend says the world will end when the cat catches that mouse.

Inside the church are many frescoes on the walls and ceiling. Over the centuries, wear and tear have taken their toll. What were once surprisingly bright colors were covered with dirt and soot. The mission's elaborate decorations are in the final stages of a restoration not unlike that performed on the Sistine Chapel. In fact, some of the experts who

San Xavier is one of the most elaborately decorated of the Jesuit missions. (Photo courtesy of Kevilee Schaich)

worked on the Sistine Chapel are involved in the work at San Xavier. This is the third restoration of this century, and the results are spectacular.

Those frescos where restoration is complete display bright and vibrant colors, quite surprising for the time and area in which they were created. Be sure to look up. The sanctuary has a domed ceiling covered with frescos, as is the high wall behind the altar. The statue of Saint Francis Xavier behind the high altar was made in Mexico City in 1759.

The view inside the Mission. Among the many frescoes, the statue of St. Francis Xavier holds a prominent place behind the altar.

San Xavier is the only Kino mission still ministering to Native Americans. Its founding is re-enacted on the first Friday after Easter. A short distance away is Grotto Hill, which is a replica of the grotto of Lourdes, and across from the church is a shop where traditional Tohono O'odham items as well as frybread can be purchased.

Sabino Canyon

Sabino Canyon is a large wilderness area on the northeast side of Tucson. It is easily accessible by auto and offers many trails, roads, streams, and canyons to hike along and explore.

Not exactly up to hiking? Don't like to walk? No problem. Sabino Canyon offers motorized tram rides up into the mountains (yes, and back again). You can drive to Sabino, park and walk fifty steps (more if you don't find the closest parking spot) to buy a ticket to the tram, ride the tram up and down the mountains, and walk fifty steps back to your car. No hiking if you don't want to.

The trams consists of perhaps five or six covered (and uncovered) jitneys, pulled by an electric car. The trams run throughout the day and are just the ticket for first-time visitors. The ranger/driver points out and names the different peaks around the canyon, identifies native vegetation, gives a bit of history, and generally helps orient you to the area. All questions are cheerfully responded to.

Buy a ticket for the tram and you can hike as much (or as little) as is comfortable and then take the tram the rest of the way up—or down. The road follows the watercourse and, depending on the time of year, water is frequently running down the stream beds. Take lots of water for drinking, your swimsuit, towel, and a picnic lunch and prepare to enjoy yourself!

There are designated stops at which you can get off to swim in a waterhole or take advantage of one of the many picnic tables scattered along the way.

Many of the trails through the Catalinas begin at the top of the roadway. The tram can save you the first 3.8 miles (all uphill) from the Visitors Center to the trail head—an easy way to start off. You can hike up into the Catalinas, explore nearby Bear Canyon, hike to the Seven Falls area (a particularly popular spot, featuring seven waterfalls when water is available), or just stay on the tram. The road is closed to any vehicular traffic except the trams.

The Santa Catalinas are rugged, rough mountains. Few of the trails through this range can be categorized as easy. For an introduction that's strenuous but not extremely so, try the trail to Hutch's Pool. The trail begins at the end of Sabino Canyon Road where the tram ride ends. It is actually the west fork of the Sabino Trail. You can hike up the road to the trail head (it's 3.8 miles past the Visitor Center) or take the tram. The first part of the trail climbs rather steeply for almost a mile (that's the strenuous part), but then sort of levels off.

The rest of the trail is a fairly easy walk, but don't stop at the first pool. Hutch's Pool is a long, narrow pool featuring a waterfall at its north end. It's a great swimming place, but be careful of hidden rocks. Diving is NOT recommended. Those who continue upstream are rewarded by several more pools. One way the trip takes about two or three hours. Allow most of the day for this relaxing and rewarding hike.

Pima Canyon Trail

Another hike recommended for those new to desert hiking is the first few miles of the Pima Canyon Trail. This is one of the most popular trails in this area. While most of it is rated as extremely difficult, the first 3.2 miles present the average hiker with much less of a challenge. From Ina Road turn north on Christie Drive. When Christie dead-ends at Magee Road, turn right and park in the signed parking area. The surrounding land is privately owned, so respect their rights.

There's a large sign proclaiming that Boy Scout Troop 211 has accepted responsibility for keeping the trail head clean. Pass this sign and follow the trail to the old jeep road. Follow the road and turn right when the trail crosses it. Keep an eye out; follow the road too far and you'll have to crawl under a fence to rejoin the trail. Soon you'll come to the Coronado National Forest entrance. Note that this is a bighorn sheep management area.

Look for the sign pointing to Mount Kimball, which is the ultimate destination of the Pima Canyon Trail. The trail climbs a bit, then levels off and heads into the mountain. Turn around occasionally; the views of Tucson are spectacular. The entire Tucson valley is visible.

The trail follows a creek bed and eventually takes you into the canyon deeply enough that the city might as well not even exist. Even if water is running, there are enough rocks to keep your feet dry. Cottonwood trees begin to provide shade. Further on the canyon opens up to Pusch Ridge. Keep an eye out! While the bighorn sheep population has declined sharply in recent years, they continue to live in the area. A sighting of one, while rare, isn't totally unheard of.

A short but steep climb is a clue that you're getting close to Pima Canyon Dam. It will probably take you two hours or so to get this far. If this marks your turnaround point, pull your lunch out of your backpack and stay awhile before starting back. Do a little exploring and you will find grinding stones (mortars) used centuries ago to grind mesquite beans carved into the bedrock in this area.

If you're a hiker, purchase Barbara Leavengood's excellent book *Hiking Trails in Tucson*. The author has hiked every trail she writes about in the book, and she gives personal and up-to-date information about what to expect.

Mount Lemon

Mount Lemmon is named after Sara Plummer Lemmon, a botanist who visited the area in 1880 while on her honeymoon. Rancher E.O. Stratton guided her and her new husband from Oracle into the Catalinas on horseback. On reaching the highest peak, the three carved their initials into a large pine and christened the peak Mount Lemmon in Sara's honor. One of the higher peaks in the Santa Catalinas at 9,157 feet of elevation, it offers a climate closer to that of Canada's than the desert.

It has long been a summer retreat for Tucsonans. The ride up along the Catalina Highway up to Windy Point, or further up to Summerhaven on Mt. Lemmon, is a pleasure. It takes less than an hour, but it can get snowy and rough in winter. Call for road information if you decide to take the ride during the winter.

The Catalina Highway begins at Tanque Verde Road on the east of Tucson. The road leads northeast up into the Catalinas and was recently renovated and reconstructed. As it goes up into the mountains, it moves through a number of life zones.

Elevation changes are used to determine life zones. A life zone is an area that supports specific plants and animals which are most suited to that elevation, weather, and range. The Catalina Highway passes through four life zones on its way up the mountain. The greatest number of cacti is found in the Lower and Upper Sonoran zones. The desert floor below 3,500 feet, which includes most of the Tucson valley, is considered the Lower Sonoran zone. This is the preferred habitat of the saguaro, for instance.

Further up the road however, on land between 3,500 feet and 6,500 feet, the saguaro is not found, although prickly pears and chollas remain. This is considered the Upper Sonoran zone, where sagebrush and piñon pine also live. When the ponderosa pine and douglas fir become common, 6,500 feet to 8,000 feet, the Transition zone has been reached. Cacti common in this zone include the claret cup and many-headed barrel cactus. Above that zone, cactus no longer grows. This is the Canadian zone, 8,000 to 9,500 feet, home to the lodgepole pine and aspen.

Today Mount Lemmon is a favorite destination for visitors and residents alike. From the intersection of Tanque Verde Road and Catalina Highway, Summerhaven is only 29.5 miles but 5,000 feet in elevation away from the desert floor. A little less than halfway up to the peak is Windy Point Vista, a well-named turnoff and lookout point. On clear days, you can see the White Dove of the Desert, San Xavier, gleaming in the distance to the southwest. A nighttime display presents the jewels of Tucson's lights competing with the stars themselves.

A little further on is Geology Vista Point. Its explanation of how the mountain was created provides interesting insight to the geology of the area, as well as a great view of the Rincon Mountains to the east. Still further, San Pedro Vista is just that: a view of the San Pedro Valley on the other side of the mountain, and you should be able to see the glint of the San Pedro River as well.

As the vegetation changes from desert to pine forest, the air becomes cooler and thinner. Campgrounds are scattered around, and some of them are next to running water. Mount Lemmon Ski Valley is a favorite stop, even if there's no snow. Weather permitting, the lift may be running, providing a spectacular view of the panorama surrounding Mount Lemmon.

Just past the turnoff to the Ski Valley is Summerhaven. The Alpine Inn is a grocery store, restaurant, and pub as well as a bed and breakfast. If you'd like to stay longer to explore the area (there's even a lake!) you may be able to find a cabin for rent. Availability is unpredictable, however. Check the business white pages in the Tucson telephone book for Mount Lemmon cabin rentals before making any firm plans.

In the winter, the skiing on Mount Lemmon attracts enthusiasts from all over southern Arizona. However, the same weather that attracts them can make the road to Mount Lemmon impassable. Call ahead to check on road conditions (Pima County Sheriff, Road Conditions, 882-2800).

> ❏ Remember that bears live all through the Catalina Mountains. If you must hike with your dog, keep it leashed. Curious dogs don't just meet bears. Javalina, bobcats, a rabid skunk, all are possible encounters. A leashed dog is a much safer one.

Colossal Cave

Colossal Cave is possibly the largest dry cavern in the world. Its interior maintains a comfortable year-round temperature of 72 degrees throughout its windings and caverns. It can be reached from either Old Spanish Trail (the scenic route) or by taking exit 279 from I-10.

When you drive up, the first thing you see (naturally) is the parking lot. Above and behind it is a large structure built entirely of natural stone against the mountain. The ramada near the cave entrance shades you until the next tour starts. Tours aren't prescheduled, and a new one begins every five to twenty minutes.

The underground tour covers about half a mile in distance and takes a little over forty-five minutes. The trail is easy, because in the mid-1930s the CCC (Civilian Conservation Corps) built the natural stone buildings, laid the walkways through the cave, and installed electric wiring. Quite an improvement over the original tours, which required not only lanterns but ropes! The original lighting has been replaced, so the only time visitors are in the dark is when (if) the guide turns the lights out.

You can take pictures inside during the tour, and the guides will be happy to tell you the best places and viewpoints. Plan on using high-speed film or a flash unit, and if you have a videocam, set it for candlelight.

Colossal Cave is a dry cave. While the extraordinary rock sculptures were formed by the dripping of mineral-rich water, the water dried up eons ago. Most other caves are wet caves, and their cave formations are still "growing." Not so in Colossal Cave. Frozen in time, these incredible geological displays of solid rock in flows, falls, and swirls are complete. The only changes that can occur now are those people might inflict on them.

Colossal Cave was known to prehistoric peoples. In 1879 it was "discovered" again and since then has been everything from an outlaw hideout in the 1800s to a movie setting (Disney's television production of *Outlaw Cats of Colossal Cave*). There are still branchings that haven't been fully explored, and no one knows how far the cave may extend, so it's highly recommended that you stay with your guide.

The cave is located inside the 500-acre Colossal Cave Park, maintained by the Pima County Parklands Foundation. Campsites are available, or bring your lunch and take advantage of the free picnic area.

Karchner Caverns

Another underground wonder, Karchner Caverns, is currently under development and unavailable for tours. It is located near Sierra Vista southeast of Tucson. The parts of the caverns so far discovered promise to offer spectacular geological wonders to spelunkers and tourists alike. The anticipated opening is scheduled for the end of 1997.

A Taste of Tucson

If you think your dining choices may be limited in Tucson, think again. Restaurants run the gamut from Pinnacle Peak, featuring steak and beans ranch house style, to the very formal and elegant Charles, where tuxedos know no shame, to a five-star restaurant, the Tack Room, that marks its entrance with a large concrete cowboy boot.

Of course, with its Mexican heritage, you expect to find Mexican food at its best. Tucson is home to some of the most inventive chefs in the country, no matter the type of food they prepare. Consult one of the locally published guides mentioned earlier for a complete listing of restaurants, including price guides.

Mexican Food

If you can't find a Mexican restaurant to your liking in Tucson you have a problem. They range from the authentic El Charro and El Minuto cafes in the downtown area to the more formal El Parador Restaurant on Broadway or La Fuente on Oracle Road, to the many family restaurants and chains scattered around the city. Here is a sampling.

To enjoy a Mexican meal in a pleasant family setting, try Molina's Midway. It's tucked away north of Speedway on Belvedere. The "Midway" in its name is all that remains of the Midway Drive-In that used to occupy the south side of Speedway. There are other Molina restaurants, operated by family members, but there's only one Molina's Midway.

What's the appeal? From the refried beans that are cooked down on the premises to the stewed tomatoes on top of the tacos, the food at Molina's Midway is much like that prepared in many households around town. This is Tucson's version of a "home cooked meal." This is a family-owned business, and some of their staff have been there for over twenty years. That sort of close-knit feeling trickles out to the customers.

Also serving Mexican food, Sanchez's Burrito Factory has branched out since beginning in 1985. In addition to the main restaurant on North Craycroft near Speedway and a smaller version near 22nd and South Craycroft, there are also several "fast-food" type outlets scattered around town.

(A burro begins with a large flour tortilla. It is spread with beans, meat, cheese—the filling defines what kind of burro it is—and then the tortilla is wrapped around the filling. These can be picked up and eaten, unless they're made "enchilada style," covered with sauce and cheese. Ummm. A "burrito" is just a smaller version of a burro.)

The name is a dead giveaway. Sanchez specializes in burritos, although in most cases they're full-fledged burros! Try the chili con carne colorado (red chili meat), but be warned that this dish is spicy. (But oh so good!) Depending on the day and time, if you visit the Speedway/Craycroft location, the mariachis may be in full voice.

The above two restaurants feature border Mexican food and represent only a bare sampling of Mexican fare available. But just as dinners in Maine differ from those served in Louisiana or Boston, there are distinct types of Mexican food. To taste Mexican food as it is served in Mexico City, La Parilla Suiza is your ticket. No tacos or enchiladas here, most entrees are charcoal grilled.

Tucson is filled with many fine Mexican restaurants, ranging from excellent to greasy, elegant to fast food, large modernized chains to family businesses that have been family-run for years. To find the one that you like best might take some time, but there's a place set for you; just bring your appetite.

Mexican Food Glossary

Before ordering, however, you may want to review what might be on the menu. Not surprisingly, when dining on Mexican food Spanish terms come in handy. You don't want to approve the addition of jalapeño peppers to a dish if you're anticipating the much milder taste of bell peppers. The following is a list of Spanish words (and their meaning) that may come in handy when reading menus.

Ajo	garlic
Albóndigas	meatballs; try sopa de albóndigas (meatball soup)
Arroz	rice
Barbacoa	barbecued meat
Borracho	cooked with wine; (means drunk)
Buñuelo	puffy, sweet, deep-fried pastry
Burro	large flour tortilla wrapped around a filling
Caliente	hot to the touch (temperature)
Camarón	shrimp
Carne	meat, specifically beef
Carne seca	dried beef jerky, shredded and spiced
Cerveza	beer
Ceviche	salad made of fish "cooked" in lime juice
Chalupa	literally, "little boat." A fried corn masa tart topped with meat, fish, beans, or vegetables
Chili powder	ground red chiles, sold in the spice department in groceries
Chimichanga	deep-fried burro; (means thingamajig)
Chorizo	spicy pork and beef sausage
Empanada	turnover
Enchilada	a corn tortilla dipped in red chile sauce, rolled around just about anything, then topped with sauce and cheese
Ensalada	salad
Flan	baked custard with caramel coating
Flauta	"flute;" deep-fried filled corn tortilla
Frijoles	literally, refried beans (pinto)
Gallina	hen
Garbanzo	chickpea
Gazpacho	spicy tomato soup, served cold
Granada	pomegranate
Habañeros	small and usually yellow or golden. Watch it, this is the hottest pepper in the world!
Harina	wheat flour
Huevo	egg; also blanquillo
Jalapeño	a dark green, very hot, pepper
Jícama	a crisp, white, edible root

Kahlúa	coffee-flavored liqueur made in Mexico
Lechuga	lettuce
Maíz	corn
Mano	a somewhat rolling-pin shaped piece of volcanic rock, held in both hands and used to grind food against a metate, a shallowly scooped out rock
Mantequilla	butter
Margarita	cocktail made with tequila and lime, served in a salt-rimmed glass. Order "sin sal" if you prefer the saltless variety
Mariscos	shellfish; fish is pescado
Masa	dough, usually ground from corn
Menudo	tripe soup; New Year's Day tradition to ease hangovers
Metate	slightly hollowed tripod rock used to grind corn
Mole	unsweetened mixture of chocolate and chile sauce
Naranja	orange
Nopales	prickly-pear cactus pads cooked and used like okra
Oja	corn husk, used to wrap tamales; sometimes hoja
Olla	clay pot
Pan	bread
Pescado	fish; shellfish is mariscos
Picante	hot (taste)
Pimienta	black pepper
Poblano	a type of chile
Pollo	chicken
Postre	dessert
Quesadilla	grilled cheese "sandwich" made with a flour tortilla
Queso	cheese
Rábano	radish
Relleno	stuffed (chili rellenos: stuffed green chilis)

Ristra	string of dried red chiles, also available in wreaths and other shapes
Sal	salt
Salsa	literally, "sauce;" usually a tomato/chili mixture of varying degrees of warmth. roceed cautiously and be warned, usually the green salsa (salsa verde) is hotter than the red (salsa rojo or salsa picante).
Sangría	a drink made of red wine, brandy, sugar, oranges, lemons, and apples
Seco	dry
Sopa	soup
Taco	a corn tortilla folded, containing various fillings
Tamal (plural is tamales)	a corn husk stuffed with masa, meat, or beans
Tequila	distilled liquor made from agave, or century plant
Topopo	a salad shaped like a volcano or pyramid
Tortilla	a thin, flat bread made from wheat flour or corn masa
Tostada	literally, "toasted;" as a menu item a crisp corn tortilla usually topped with a mixture of beans, meat, lettuce, tomatoes, and cheese

Spanish rules of pronunciation are consistent (unlike English).

Vowels:	a as in "father"
	e as in "effort"
	i and y as in "taxi"
	o as in "gold"
	u as in "cool"

Spanish consonants are pronounced the same as in English, with a few exceptions:

> ñ — "ny" as in "canyon"
> ll — like "y" in English
> s and z sound alike
> c before e, i, or y sounds like s
> c before other vowels sounds like k
> ch is always hard, as in "church"

Chili First Aid

An ingredient that plays a sometimes exciting element in Mexican food is the chili pepper. Chilis range a great amount in their degree of "hotness." The fire in the peppers comes from capsaicin, and Mexican food is full of the stuff. Whether by intent or accident, if you happen to take a bite of something just a *little* too warm for your taste or you added a touch too much hot sauce, **Drink milk!** The higher the butterfat content the better. Whole milk is good, half-and-half is better, sour cream is wonderful.

Forget ice water—it doesn't work and might even spread that too-hot feeling to other parts of your mouth. Sugar will help (that's right, pour it right in), but milk is usually all you need.

Fine Dining

Tucson takes a back seat to no city in its array of fine restaurants, with a selection ranging from a five-star restaurant to the four-star resorts dotting the foothills to one of the superb valley eateries.

One of Tucson's more unique restaurants is Janos, owned by chef Janos Wilder. Located downtown at 150 North Main Avenue, Janos' food blends Continental cuisine with Southwestern style and flavors. The meals at Janos are dependent on both the season and availability of ingredients, many of which are purchased from local gardeners.

Janos (real name John) is a well-known chef, not just in Tucson, but nationwide. His background includes restaurants in Boulder and Gold Hill, Colorado, Santa Fe, New Mexico, and Bordeaux, France. In 1983 when the Tucson Museum of Art was renovating a historic building, the Hiram Stevens House, Janos learned they would consider leasing it as a restaurant. On October 31, 1983, Janos opened for business, and today it is one of Tucson's four diamond restaurants.

When the weather is good (when isn't it?) try dining al fresco on the terrace. Don't let the wonderful food distract you, however, from the beauty of this restored home. It originally included an aviary, orchard, carriage house, and stables. The pepper tree at the front door was planted by the original owner, Hiram Stevens.

Charles is another restaurant located in a restored home, but this English manor home is as far from Janos' frontier adobe as you can imagine. Happily, however, the cuisine here is equally fine. A hidden treasure, take Wilmot north from Speedway. Stay to the right and turn on El Dorado Circle (you'll be going east) and follow the road, which is shaded by cypress trees. The exact address is 6400 East El Dorado Circle.

Last but not least on our short list is the Tack Room. Hard to miss driving down Sabino Canyon Drive (just look for the big boot), the Tack Room has been a hometown favorite for many years. It's a five-star restaurant located in a home that was converted to a dude ranch and quarter horse ranch.

There are any number of fine dining establishments from the Gold Room at the Westward Look Resort, the Ventana Room at Loews Ventana Resort, to steak houses done the Southwestern style (mesquite broiled), to Anthony's, known for its seafood, to chain restaurants. You'll find no limitations in Tucson.

Entertainment

To really get a sense of what's going on in our fair city, we suggest you find a copy of the *Tucson Weekly*. This is a free paper, that also an up-to-the-week guide to everything. Published every Thursday, you'll find it in stands all over the city. Check the libraries, but you have to move fast! It's gone almost as soon as it's dropped off. If it's happening in Tucson, it's in the *Weekly*. Admittedly, some of the articles and advertisements are geared to extremes, but at the same time you can find out mundane things such as where to have lunch for under $5.00. Two other publications, mentioned previously, that are indispensable for finding out what's happening in Tucson and the surrounding area are the *Tucson Official Visitors Guide* and the *Tucson Guide Quarterly*.

Touring Tucson

Orienting yourself in Tucson is fairly easy. The Catalinas, practically always easy to see, are on the north side of town. "Streets" run east and west, and "Avenues" run north and south. There are boulevards and roads that can run any way they please. You'll see some Mexican names for streets: Calle (pronounced "ka yay" and abbreviated on maps as "C"), Camino (CMO), Caminito (CTO), Avenidas (AVE), Vias, and others. Stone Avenue is the dividing line for addresses running east and west; Broadway Boulevard is the dividing line between north and south addresses. This can be rather confusing because First Street is more than one block north of Broadway, and the number names of the streets don't exactly follow the numbers of the north or south addresses. For example, Broadway starts counting 1 south, but it's where 11th Street should be according to street names.

Want to get a little more confused? When you're on the east side of the city, that is, east of Stone, streets that run east and west have odd numbers on the north side of the street and even numbers on the south. When you're west of Stone, the east-west streets have odd numbers on the south side of the street and even numbers on the north. Likewise, when you're north of Broadway, odd numbers are on the west side of the street and even numbers on the east. When you're south of Broadway, odd numbers are on the east side of the street and even numbers are on the west side.

The major east-west streets 22nd Street, Broadway, Speedway, and Grant are about one mile apart. The same holds true for the major north-south streets: Stone, Campbell, Country Club, Alvernon, Swan, Craycroft, Wilmot, Kolb, and Pantano are all about a mile apart.

Downtown Tucson is a hub of the business community. The government buildings are there, along with major office

Downtown Tucson houses many government and business offices. The University of Arizona lies to the north and east. (Photo courtesy of Kevilee Schaich)

buildings. It seems to be like most downtowns areas, very active during the business week and rather empty during the weekends. Many of the streets in the downtown area are one-way only, so check the signs before making a turn.

Speaking of one-ways streets, pay attention to some parts of Grant Road and Broadway Boulevard. During most of the day they contain five lanes, two each heading east and west and a center lane for left turns. But during rush hour, between 7:00 and 9:00 a.m. and 4:00 and 6:00 p.m. the center left turn lane becomes a traffic lane carrying traffic west into downtown in the mornings, and east out of downtown in the afternoons. No left turns are permitted. This arrangement is only in effect on weekdays in certain areas, and it is clearly marked with overhead lights and signage. Again, check the signs. Trying to make a left-hand turn from this lane during those times is practically asking to be bulldozed!

The city first developed from the downtown area eastward, running along the south face of the Catalinas. Central and Midtown neighborhoods run east of downtown along the path between 22nd Street on the south and Grant Road on the north. The Central area is around the university. Midtown is, well, the middle of the town. As you continue east along Broadway there's El Con Mall, office buildings and strip shops, the Williams Center, and then Park Mall.

The further north you go, the neighborhoods back up into the Catalina mountains. The land becomes quite hilly and steeper (and more expensive) the further north you go. The Catalina foothills feature custom homes, dramatic mountain settings and desert vegetation, and nighttime views of the city. It's a fairly pricey neighborhood. The further up the mountain you go, the pricier it is.

When you travel northeast you'll find Sabino Canyon in the Coronado National Forest, which encompasses much of the Santa Catalina Mountains. Further east along Tanque Verde Road is Redington Pass leading to Redington and San Manuel, over the mountains. Turning the corner to the Rincons the land flattens out into desert and homes become farther apart. You see ranches and horses until you're suddenly bumping into the Rincon Mountains and Saguaro National Park-East, where the roads all come to an end.

In recent years, development has gone to the opposite sides of town, north and west. Most new homes are being built on the north side of town, west of where the Catalinas suddenly come to an end. The northwest side of the city is growing the fastest now. A number of new subdivisions and developments have sprung up, along with retirement communities, shopping centers, medical centers, and resorts. This is the area that runs north along Oracle Road, contains the Tucson Mall, the largest shopping mall in Tucson, and leads into Oro Valley and further on to Biosphere 2.

Westside homes are in the foothills of the Tucson Mountains. There are many open spaces and a gradual elevation as you head west. It offers a panoramic view of the city and the Catalinas. Fifteen or twenty minutes of driving from I-10 takes you into the Tucson Mountain Park, Gate's Pass, the Arizona-Sonora Desert Museum, Old Tucson, and Saguaro National Park-West.

The southwestern section of Tucson borders the San Xavier Indian Reservation and has a lot of open desert. To the southeast is the industrial corridor with Hughes, Burr Brown, and other businesses. Tucson International Airport is also located here. Travel further east along I-10 and you reach the 1,000,000 square foot, former IBM complex, that now houses more Hughes offices, Microsoft's service center, and a branch of the University of Arizona.

Historic Tucson

Tucson is quite proud of its history. One of the indications of this is the effort the Tucson/Pima County Historical Commission has made to preserve the city's landmark historic buildings. They have established six districts in Tucson that are listed in the National Register of Historic Places: Four of these districts are downtown or near the university, the fifth is just west of the El Con Mall, and the sixth is in the Fort Lowell area. They are protected by national or city historic status. Walking tours are available going through the Barrio Historico, El Presidio Historico, and Armory Park Districts for a closer encounter with the history of the area.

El Presidio Historico

The first district is called El Presidio. It is the original location of the Old Pueblo, and is bounded approximately by Alameda and 6th Street, and Church and Granada avenues.

The southern half of the original presidio was known as the Plaza de Las Armas. Here soldiers drilled and practiced military formation, and residents gathered for fiestas and public events. Now it is the center of Tucson's government. Modern Tucsonans also hold their Tucson Meet Yourself evenings in El Presidio Park. The Plaza has shade trees, sculptures, and bubbling fountains. On the east is the Pima County Courthouse, to the south are Pima County office buildings, and City Hall is on the west. The Federal Building is to the west and south.

The original presidio had only one entry which was located at what is now the intersection of Alameda and Main Avenue. Its adobe walls, approximately ten to twelve feet tall and three feet wide at the base, enclosed barracks, the military chapel of San Agustín, a well, a cemetery, a granary, stables, some plazas, and storage buildings.

Iron bolts on a massive mesquite door kept out danger. It was bolted at night and, of course, during Indian raids. The sentry kept guard on a platform above the gate, and an Indian guard stood watch from the top of Sentinel Peak ("A" Mountain) some distance away.

The Tucson Museum of Art complex, 140 N. Main, encompasses the northern portion of the original presidio. All historic buildings are listed on the National Register of Historic Places. There are walking tours available to gather more complete information about these homes and buildings. They give us a good idea of what it was like to live in Tucson at the turn of the century.

The Edward Nye Fish House, 120 N. Main, holds some interesting history. It was built in 1868 with fifteen-foot-high ceilings to allow the hot air to rise above the living area. Its carpeting was laid over dirt floors first tamped down and covered with burlap. Mr. Fish was the owner of one of the largest businesses in the territory and owned the city's first steam-powered flour mill. His wife, Maria Wakefield, was the first Anglo woman to be married in Tucson. She was a schoolteacher who came to Tucson from Stockton, California with another female teacher. Their trek to Tucson involved going by train from Stockton to San Francisco, steamer from there to San Diego, then by stagecoach to Tucson. They arrived in November 1873, and school opened two days later.

Another historic house in the area is the Stevens House, at 150 N. Main. Life on the frontier was not always nice. Hiram Stevens was a successful businessman and rancher. His wife, Petra Santa Cruz, was the granddaughter of his Mexican servant. Coming from a peasant home and a life of privation, she became associated through her husband with Tucson society. In 1893 a drought killed most of Steven's cattle and he had other business setbacks. He shot his wife and then killed himself. But Petra was lucky. The bullet glanced off the Spanish comb she used to hold back her hair and only wounded her slightly. She eventually recovered and moved to California. The restored Steven's home is now occupied by the Janos Restaurant.

The Levi Manning House is also in this area at 450 W. Paseo. It was built in 1897. It is located in an area called "Snob Hollow." You guessed it, that's where all the rich people lived. Manning came to Tucson in 1884. He was a mine owner, a newspaper reporter, a merchant and builder, and served as mayor in 1905 to 1907.

The J. Knox Corbett House is also located in Snob Hollow at 180 N. Main. Knox was a South Carolina native who moved here in 1880. He sold newspapers, was a clerk in his brother's store, and worked at the post office. He eventually went into the lumber business and owned stage lines and ranches. He was mayor of Tucson from 1914 until 1917. Knox married the oldest daughter of Atanacia Santa Cruz and Sam Hughes. Atanacia was the sister of Petra Santa Cruz whose Spanish comb saved her life.

The Cordova House at 175 N. Meyer Avenue is an excellent example of an 1880s Tucson house. The homes were built right on the street. There was no front lawn or sidewalk. The patio in the rear of the house was used for cooking. No extra heat was inside the house in the desert. Well water was used for cooking and cleaning only. Drinking water was purchased from the city of Tucson. With little wood available, the house was built with dirt and cactus. Adobes are mud bricks, made of clay, sand, and a binder of straw. The mixture is shoveled into forms and left to dry for two to three weeks. Adobe is an excellent insulator and kept the heat out in the summer, and the cold out in winter. The floor was dirt. It was sprinkled with water, swept, and tamped down daily. Ceilings were made from saguaro ribs sometimes supported by pine beams and packed with mud over a foot thick. The flat roof was slightly tilted so the rain water could drain off without taking the roof with it.

This style of building, called the "territorial," is very common in modern Tucson. No, not the mud floors, ceilings, and roofs! However, you will find many homes in Tucson made of adobe bricks, often a couple of feet thick, with small windows on the front, one story high, and with flat roofs. There are often arched windows and covered patios around the perimeter of the houses. Rather than garages which tend to hold heat, many homes have car ports instead.

On the northeast corner of Washington and Main is the Sam Hughes House. (It is now a series of apartments and not too easy to recognize.) Sam Hughes is a well-known name in Tucson. He was born in Wales and moved to Pennsylvania with his family in 1837. He moved to California with many other gold seekers in 1850 and moved to Tucson in 1858 after he was injured in a mine. He was reportedly the sixth Anglo to live in Tucson. He organized the first bank and school, was one of the incorporators of the city as a municipality, and served as an alderman for seven years. One of Tucson's most popular neighborhoods (just west of El Con Mall) is named for him.

He was a business associate of Hiram Stevens and eventually married Atanacia Santa Cruz, the sister of Stevens' wife. They were married at San Xavier Mission in 1862. Their marriage lasted over fifty years, and they had fifteen children. Sam Hughes was one of the participants in the Camp Grant Massacre.

The Julius Kauttschnitt home is at 297 Main Street and is thought to have been originally built in the 1880s. It first had a flat roof of adobe and a veranda. The rooms had high ceilings and opened into a twelve-foot-wide center hall that led to the rear garden and patio. It had a gabled roof, a widow's walk, and Victorian trim added later. The Kauttschnitts moved here in 1912. He was a Yale graduate, and his wife was the daughter of a San Francisco real estate developer. It has been totally refurbished and is now the El Presidio Bed and Breakfast Inn.

Across the street and down the block from the Kauttschnitt home at 378 N. Main is the Steinfeld Mansion. This was no adobe brick house. It was built of brick stucco in the Spanish mission style. It was originally designed to house several bachelors in 1899 and was known as the Owl's Club. Albert and Bettina Steinfeld purchased the home in 1904 and renovated it. It included parquet floors, tile framed fireplaces, and Oriental carpets. At the rear is a patio area, a small garden, and a two-story wooden porch with double bannisters. It was the showplace of Tucson and was decorated with mahogany and included Chinese teakwood antiques. The home had the first bathtub with running water in Tucson. Tucson's public bathhouses soon closed as other houses in the city installed indoor plumbing.

There are over twenty-five historic buildings and homes in the El Presidio area. On South Stone Avenue you'll find present-day St. Augustine Cathedral. (Remember that Tucson's full name was once San Agustín del Tucson.) It was originally constructed in 1896 and remodeled in the 1920s. In 1967 it was enlarged and now is in the cathedral style of European churches.

Barrio Historico

Another historical district is directly south of downtown and the Tucson Convention Center. It is known as the Barrio (the neighborhood). Other names are Barrio Historico (historic), Barrio Libre (free), and Barrio Viejo (old). It acquired these names in the wild days of the 1800s when this part of town was independent of the rest of the area and paid little heed to the laws. El Minuto Cafe, an excellent Mexican restaurant on South Main Avenue, the Cushing Street Bar, and office buildings serve to buffer the area. Also in this area next to El Minuto is the wishing shrine of El Tiradito.

Armory Park

The Armory Park district is to the east of the Barrio. It was developed with the arrival of the railroad in the 1880s and was the home of a number of affluent and working-class citizens of the time. Its boundaries are approximately 12th Street on the north, 19th Street on the south, 3rd Avenue on the east, and Stone Avenue on the west.

The turn of the century brought more American tastes to Tucson. Wooden roofs and porches began appearing on houses built in the Armory Park area. There were tract homes built as well as custom homes. You can see here homes in the style you might be familiar with if you grew up in cities of the Midwest and East.

University of Arizona Campus

Another historic district is the University of Arizona Campus historic district. There are eighteen historic buildings here as well as a fountain and the wall that served as the perimeter of the original university. Its black volcanic stones were gathered from Sentinel Peak and give you a clear indication why "black mountain" is part of Tucson's name.

The West University Historic District is south of Speedway and continues to East 6th Street. Its east and west borders are Tyndall Avenue and Stone. There are historic homes of all styles here, including Victorian and Queen Anne, California bungalows, Pueblo Revival, and Tudor Revival styles.

One of the houses here is the Ronstadt House. It was designed by Henry Trost, one of the first architects who lived in Tucson and who developed an excellent reputation. Fred Ronstadt built the home in 1903 but sold it in 1920 before his famous daughter Linda was born.

Here on North Second Avenue was also the hideout of John Dillinger and his gang. Tucson police captured him and three of his gang members here. They were sent back to Chicago where Dillinger eventually escaped, only to be gunned down by police outside of a movie theater.

One interesting aside: In July 1970 Speedway Boulevard, a major east-west thoroughfare in Tucson, was named by *Life* magazine as the "Ugliest Street in America." At the time there were innumerable billboards, business signs, and other unattractive blemishes sometimes known as buildings lining the boulevard. Harold Steinfeld (see Steinfeld Mansion on page 135) and Barney Oldfield (one of America's most famous early automobile racers) helped give the street its name originally by racing their cars along what was then just a dirt track leading out into the desert. How things change. Today Speedway has dressed itself up and is no longer the butt of jokes.

El Encanto Estates

El Encanto Estates is on the National Register of Historic Places more because of its layout and landscaping than because of its homes. It lies east of Country Club Road and just west of the El Con Mall. It was developed in 1928 and has circular and diagonal streets, cul-de-sacs, and a central, circular park. Mexican fan palms were planted along the streets, and 157 saguaros are planted in its central park.

Fort Lowell Historic Neighborhood

The Fort Lowell Historic Neighborhood is located just west of Fort Lowell Park at Craycroft and Fort Lowell. It has a distinct rural flavor as it was once the site of an agricultural center. The Rillito River formed by the Pantano and Tanque Verde rivers once flowed through the area. It still does, but only after a healthy rain. In the early 1900s the neighborhood was to the west of Fort Lowell. It's now known as El Fuerte (the fort). Food from the farms was sold in Tucson and to the military. A small chapel, San Pedro, is currently being rehabilitated.

Other Neighborhoods

If you look in newspaper advertisements for houses, sooner or later you'll come across the name "Joesler." You often see the name mentioned in real estate listings. Josias Joesler was an architect who designed many homes in Tucson from 1927 until 1956. It's sort of funny that Joesler is known as a famous architect in Tucson, because he designed homes that were of the style of buildings in other parts of the West.

Joesler was born in Switzerland and attended engineering and architecture schools there, in Germany, and also at the Sorbonne in Paris. His travels eventually led to Los Angeles where he met John and Helen Murphy, real estate developers. They were building residential communities in Tucson to attract wealthy residents from both California and the East. They wanted an architect who could design buildings that portrayed the various styles popular in other areas of the West. The Murphys built many subdivisions here, and Joesler designed and supervised the construction of them. Catalina Foothills Estates is one of the better known developments. The majority of the homes are centered around a patio or pool and have low-pitched tile roofs. There are many archways, breezeways, and patios.

Many of the homes in that elite subdivision were in the Spanish Colonial Revival style, but Joesler was really an eclectic. Some of the other homes he designed were in Santa Fe, contemporary ranch, art deco, and other styles which were often blended together. Since the homes were all custom-built, it is not surprising that there are still over two hundred of them in the town today.

The University of Arizona

The University of Arizona is one of Tucson's shining lights. It is a world-renowned university, a significant source of income for the city, has attracted businesses and industry to Tucson, and provides much entertainment and sports for Tucson's citizens. The university is spread out but generally contained within the boundaries formed by Euclid Street on the west, Sixth Avenue on the south, Campbell Avenue on the east, and Speedway Boulevard on the north.

The university wasn't always welcomed. When C.C. Stephens returned from the Thirteenth Territorial Legislature with the news that Tucson had been awarded the university, the good citizens of Tucson pelted him with decayed produce, rotten eggs, and (by some accounts) at least one dead cat.

The reason for their pique? Stevens had been sent to Prescott not to secure a university, but to gain the capital status which had been lost to Prescott in 1877. Money also played a part in their dismay. Up for grabs had been the university, a teachers' college, an insane asylum, and the capital designation. Unfortunately, most of the horse trading had taken place long before Stephens even reached Prescott. The upshot was that Prescott retained the capital, Tempe got the teachers' college (Arizona Territorial Normal School) and $5,000, Phoenix was awarded the asylum (and $100,000), and lowly Tucson was stuck with the university and a measly $25,000.

Tucsonans were not impressed. There was not even one high school in the area, and the common citizen had more in mind than education. One man of the day is quoted as saying, "Who ever knew a perfesser to order a drink?" Nevertheless, if it hadn't been for the owner of Tucson's finest saloon and two gamblers, the University of Arizona might have died unborn. These gentlemen, E.C. Gifford, B.C. Parker, and W.S. Reid ("Billy" Reid was the saloon owner) donated the forty acres of land on which the first buildings of the Territorial University (today's University of Arizona) would be built. Apparently there was some arm-twisting involved, but the transfer was accomplished and the deed recorded on November 27, 1886.

The ground hadn't even been broken, however, before the fledgling institution had to fight off two potentially lethal attacks. The first battle was joined during the Fourteenth Legislature, when representatives of Cochise County attempted to repeal the University Act, thus making its $25,000 fair game. Only sketchy reports are available of what must have been a fiery session, but in the end Pima County defeated the attempt.

The next ambush came from within. Tucson citizens wanted $10,000 of the university funds used to develop an artesian well. What with one thing and another, the ground-breaking wasn't held until October 27, 1887. The School of Mines (now known as Old Main) was the first building erected. The regents performed near miracles in making the original $25,000 stretch to meet their needs. The building was sunk six feet into the ground to save money on its support and first floor walls.

Old Main at the University of Arizona.

Running out of money despite their best efforts, the regents returned to the Legislature and convinced the body politic to pass a three-quarter mil tax. This would have been very useful, but the body politic decided at that point to have a family spat. The governor then declined to sign any of the last eleven bills passed, and the university tax bill was one of them.

While the case of the "lost bills" was taken to court and the bills validated, the university remained without a roof. Not without resources, the regents invented a School of Agriculture in 1889. There was no building, no faculty, and no money, but the school was substantial enough to receive $10,000 in federal funds. The next year they qualified for $25,000 in federal funds and an additional $15,000 from the state legislature. In 1897 the university received its first research grant, $10,000 from the Copper Queen Company to be spent for instruments or equipment for the School of Mines.

October 1, 1891 was the university's first day, opening with a faculty of six to a first student body of thirty-two, offering two curricula—agriculture and mining.

One problem the university faced, particularly in the early years, was the sad fact that all their students were not of university caliber. In 1891 the Arizona Territory boasted not one high school, and there were no uniform courses of study for the elementary levels. The only hope parents had to educate their children was the university, and they tried to enroll so many thirteen-year-olds, the university had to set fourteen as the minimum age for admission.

Of the original thirty-two first semester students, only six were able to enter as university freshmen. The other twenty-six were given preparatory course work. Even so, half the freshmen dropped out in the first three months. Considering the by-and-large lack of primary education in the Arizona Territory in the 1890s, that's not too bad. On May 29, 1895, the university's first three graduates received diplomas.

It took seventeen years before there were more university than preparatory students, and twenty-three years until the preparatory classes were abolished. Twenty-five faculty members resigned in the first ten years, but those who took their places and those who stayed were determined to see that the Territorial University offer the highest quality education possible. If this meant they had to act as a high school for a few years, so be it.

From the beginning the university has been and is much more than an opportunity for students, carrying out its three-fold mission of teaching, research, and public service. The university's expertise, background, and other resources have always been available to the entire state (then Territory) of Arizona. The very first report the regents made (December 1892) suggested offering extension courses for more mature people throughout the Arizona Territory.

The School of Mines not only taught mining and engineering but offered practical help to miners and mine owners, ranging from improved mining techniques to more economical ore treatments. The school's first report regretted not having the staff to systematically survey Arizona's mineral resources. Still in its first year, the School of Agriculture offered soil and water tests, testing fattening cattle feeds, and had visited nearly every irrigation system in the territory.

It was just this attitude that put the university in the forefront of bringing Arizona into the modern world. It wasn't enough just to teach courses. From its inception the university has provided direct benefits to Arizona citizens. The School of Agriculture began experimental agricultural stations to work on such problems as irrigation, range land reclamation, and crop yield. A series of bulletins and leaflets was also published and saw wide distribution. Not to be outdone, the School of Mines began offering "at-cost" assay tests much more cheaply than commercial assayers did.

(In the 1920s, Nellie Bush—future pilot, lawyer, and steamboat captain—was a law student at the University of Arizona. At the time, university policy required women students to leave the classroom when the case under discussion involved rape. The policy was changed when Nellie inquired of the dean if he knew of any rape case that didn't involve a woman.)

Today the University of Arizona offers courses in everything from liberal and fine arts to mining and medicine leading to degrees of bachelor, master, and doctor. The university oversees ten agricultural-research centers, and future archaeologists receive field experience and research and training opportunities at off-campus sites. Two on-campus museums offer fine art and photographic exhibitions, both temporary and changing, as well as research archives, educational programs, and other benefits. Other on-campus attractions include the Poetry Center, Flandrau Planetarium, and Science Center and Mineral Museum.

The University of Arizona Extended University offers a wide variety of options. A number of the noncredit personal development courses focus on the Southwest, providing new residents or visitors with an introduction to the crafts, arts, history, and architecture of our area. The Extended University also hosts TravelLearn tours, guided to destinations around the world by both university faculty and on-site specialists. Three Elderhostel programs are offered at Tucson, Nogales, and the White Stallion Ranch.

Exploring the University Today

Visitor Center

Your first stop might well be the university visitor center, on the north side of Cherry Avenue and University Boulevard. Here is a wealth of information about the university, including maps and brochures detailing the various sites of interest. However, much of the university is set up for foot and bicycle traffic only, so the parking garage just south of the center may be your first destination. (The university library is across the street to the west.)

When the university began, it was way out in the boonies from Tucson proper. At one time the natural stone wall still visible along Park marked the university's boundaries. Now, while Tucson surrounds the campus on all sides, the university itself stretches far beyond our valley. Considering its involvement in the Hubble Space Telescope and the upcoming Mars mission, the university really no longer has any boundaries.

Old Main

Visitors touring the university's campus will note the lavish use of red brick that marks many structures, particularly the older buildings. This is particularly noticeable entering the campus going east on University from Park. If you enter the campus from here, "Old Main" will be directly ahead. Built on what was a mesquite-covered mesa east of Tucson, this center of the original university features the original fountain.

Museum of Art

Other on-campus destinations for visitors include the University of Arizona Museum of Art. Here is one of the most complete university collections of Renaissance and later European and American art in the Southwest. The permanent collection consists of a wide variety of paintings, sculptures, drawings, and prints. Both classical and modern artists such as Picasso and O'Keeffe are represented. Some part of the permanent collection is always on view in addition to constantly changing temporary exhibitions. The museum offers tours, discussion groups, performances, and lectures as part of its educational activities. With two week's notice gallery tours can be scheduled, and they also give a variety of art appreciation and interpretation programs.

Center for Creative Photography

If photography as art is more to your liking, visit the Center for Creative Photography. This combination museum and research center is devoted to photography as an art form, and constitutes the world's largest repository of photographic images. Housing the prints and negatives of more than 1,500 nineteenth and twentieth century photographers, including Ansel Adams, the center was born in

1974 subsequent to an agreement between then university president Dr. John P. Schaefer and Ansel Adams. Adams' sole condition in allowing the university possession of his life's work was that the archives would remain available to the public for research and study.

While appointments are necessary for scholars wanting to peruse the collections of such photographers as Adams, Aaron Siskind, and Paul Strand, the casual visitor is welcomed to the main gallery. Exhibits change periodically and may feature the center's own works or traveling exhibits from other galleries. Visitors also have access to the center's reading and print viewing rooms, as well as a museum shop.

Poetry Center

The Poetry Center is located at 1216 North Cherry. In 1960 writer-editor Ruth Stephan gave the university two historic adobe houses and a small endowment "to maintain and cherish the spirit of poetry." The intervening thirty-six years has seen her gift become a national literary resource.

The center's poetry collection consists of over 26,000 books, periodicals, recordings (both audio and visual), photographs, broadsides, and artist-designed and limited edition books. Since 1962 the center has hosted a free reading series featuring major U.S. poets, international visitors, new, experimental, and innovative writers, and U of A faculty and student poets. The center also has a guest house for visiting writers, and it supports several workshops in the Southern Arizona area.

Special Places and Unique Customs

Now that you can find your way there and back, we want to show you a few places around Tucson that are special.

El Tiradito

An exclusive Tucson piece of history that's now inextricably mixed with legend is the wishing shrine of El Tiradito (el tier-ah-dé-to), or the castaway. It's the only national shrine in the U.S. dedicated to a sinner who was buried in unconsecrated ground.

El Tiradito. This small shrine is a favorite spot for those who have special wishes.

The shrine is dedicated to a young man buried where he fell. He was killed as a consequence of his involvement with a married woman. Stories differ, but in 1927 the Tucson city council accepted the following version, told them by a sheep rancher.

A rancher hired a young herder and his father-in-law to work for him. The younger man, Juan, became involved in an affair with his mother-in-law. When the pair were discovered in bed, the father-in-law chased the young man out of the house, picked up an ax, and killed him with it. The father-in-law took off for places unknown. Juan was buried where he died, at what is now the intersection of Meyer and Simpson streets.

When Simpson Street was lengthened, the shrine and grave were moved to their present location, just south of El Minuto Mexican restaurant at 354 South Main Avenue. In 1940 the site was cleared of trash and the existing three-sided wall built by the NYA (National Youth Administration).

Somehow over the years the site has become a shrine. If you visit, you'll notice the abundance of candle wax and, depending on when you arrive, candles. There are at least two traditions involving candles at El Tiradito. Some light a candle for a specific request. According to some, if your candle stays lit all night, your prayer will be answered. Others believe that lighting a candle on the last or first day of the year brings good luck to their new year.

Tia Elena

If you drive past 3402 Grant Road, look for Tia Elena (Aunt Helen) on the south side of the road. This elegant concrete creation once beckoned diners into a Mexican restaurant. Now she graces the front of Tom's Used Furniture and Collectibles.

The restaurant started out in the 1960s in an adobe house at the southeast corner. Success allowed it to branch out, and two separate houses were joined and now constitute the east-west wings of the current building. When they were joined by a common wall, Tia Elena was created. When the current owner purchased the building, he planned to remove Auntie. Unfortunately, investigation showed that she's such an integral part of the structure that to evict her, the entire wall and part of the roof would have to be demolished. So Tia Elena lives on.

Tia Elena. Notice the nearby saguaro complete with holes. These are nesting sites, which are used from year to year.

La Llorona

La Llorona (la yer-oh-nah), or the Crying Woman, is an old Southwestern tale. As with most cultures, mothers often have to call their children to come home. As children do, some ignore those calls. After calling two or three times, Tucson mothers finally might call out "Get in here before La Llorona finds you!" Tucson kids get.

La Llorona is a woman who had murdered her children years ago by drowning them in a river. She went mad because of the murders and her grief. Now she wanders the land, crying and wailing, looking for her lost children, taking any child she can find. Because she is both mad and a spirit, any child might be taken to replace one of her lost ones. Especially in the evenings, she might snatch one up and it would be gone forever! A great way to keep kids in line.

The story of La Llorona is known, seen, and heard throughout Mexico, indeed, much of South as well as North America, anywhere Hispanic peoples have settled. It isn't exclusively a Tucson legend. The specifics of her crime, appearance, and the actual danger she poses may change from one locale to another, but the legend of La Llorona is a permanent part of Tucson's oral folklore.

El Con Water Tower

On the south side of Broadway near Randolph Way, across from the El Con Mall, is a tall sand-colored tower. This tall structure, topped with the cut-out figure of a prospector leading a well-provisioned burro toward the western horizon, is actually a four-sided false front known as the El Con Water Tower.

After the First World War, Tucson became a favorite winter destination. The twenty-room El Conquistador Resort stood near Broadway and Alvernon, where the El Con Mall is today. Only one building remains and can still be seen. Water has always been a primary concern in Tucson, and in 1928 a standard steel water tower was built to serve the needs of not only the resort, but two subdivisions in the area.

After vocal complaints by neighbors, in 1932 a chicken-wire and plaster enclosure was built to conceal the steel tower. It was actively used by Tucson Water Company until 1970. It is the only enclosed water tower in Arizona. It won a listing on the National Register of Historic Places in 1980

The El Con Water Tower. This structure is a facade hiding an ordinary water tower.

and was named an official historic landmark by the Tucson City Council in 1991. The structure was completely restored in 1994.

Kokopelli

Kokopelli isn't an exclusively Tucson image, but this seems a good place to talk about him. Another trickster, similar to Coyote, he's usually described as a humpbacked flute player who interacts with humans in unexpected ways. The Kokopelli image is seen in ancient Hohokam and Anasazi/Pueblo petroglyphs as well as at modern craft shows. Many earlier images are emphatically masculine, but the modern Kokopelli seems less enthusiastic. Archeologists have also alternatively explained his humped back as a peddlar's pack.

Tohono Chul Park

If the word "park" conjures up mental images of rolling lawns shaded by tall trees, perhaps with a small stream running through, Tohono Chul Park will surprise you. Yes, there's a stream, but Tohono Chul is a desert park. There are trees, palo verdes and mesquite, but no grass. Next to one of the busiest streets in Tucson, once within its thirty-seven acres the entire world recedes. It is located near the intersection of Oracle and Ina Road. This is an opportunity to visit the desert without leaving the city to do so, in a comfortable, accessible setting.

Richard and Jean Wilson, owners of the Haunted Bookshop (located on the property), created Tohono Chul as a gift to the people of Tucson. The name is from the Tohono O'odham language, and means "desert corner." Beginning in 1966, they began acquiring what eventually became a thirty-seven-acre parcel. In 1979 they began building a path, which eventually grew into a half-mile loop through the desert. To ensure that the beauty of Tohono Chul would be available to future visitors, a nonprofit foundation was created in the 1980s to manage the park.

Guided tours and bird-watching walks are held on a weekly basis. Conducted by docents, these are free to members of Tohono Chul Park. A two-dollar donation is suggested for nonmembers. Bird walks and other tours can also be arranged by calling the park. One of its most popular events comes on July nights. The night blooming cereus is a cactus that blooms only at night. It has very beautiful and ephemeral flowers. When the cactus gets ready to bloom, it brings out a crowd hoping that the cactus will open one of its fragrant buds in their presence. The buds only last a few hours, but it's a magical experience.

You're also welcome to walk yourself through the park. There are a number of resting spots, one by a (recirculating) stream. The park's botanical gardens allow you to identify a variety of plants (a boojum tree, perhaps?). The geology exhibits introduce you firsthand to the Catalina Mountains. Both nature trails at Tohono Chul are wheelchair accessible. Strategically placed ramadas cast welcome shade for both walkers and those taking advantage of the picnic tables.

Many different gardens dot the grounds. The garden for children invites the younger set to explore and learn. Tools such as a weather station and peer-o-scope mingle with topiary animals, a maze, and bird houses. The Alice Holsclaw Performance Garden hosts many concerts, lectures, and other events held at the park. Don't miss the hummingbird garden, designed to attract these jewels of the air. In fact, the entire park is intended as an "aviary without walls." Birds as diverse as cardinals, hawks, and roadrunners make their home here.

For residents interested in successful desert gardening, the demonstration garden features plants and landscaping materials that are suited for Tucson's climate. In the greenhouse, visitors to Tohono Chul can ask questions, receive advice, and purchase desert plants and other gardening items.

If you'd rather not bring your lunch, the Tohono Chul Tea Room serves breakfast and lunch, as well as high tea. Sit and enjoy your meal in one of the two patios. The enclosed patio offers the sound of water from its fountain, or dine in the open patio and watch cactus wrens arguing against a mountain backdrop. An old adobe house in the park is used to present an ever-changing display of art exhibits, while the two gift shops on the premises offer unique items with a Southwestern flavor.

Reid Park Zoo

One of the smaller zoos in the country, Reid Park Zoo is a hidden treasure. Tucked away in Reid Park (some still call it Randolph Park), this zoo emphasizes natural environments for its residents. Visit residents of the Australian outback, the grasslands of Asia, and an African veldt while strolling along a (partially) shaded walkway. You may have to look closely to see the pigmy hippopotamus in her pool. There's also a great waterfowl display, including both fish and fowl, as well as the lions, tigers, and bears all zoo-goers expect to see.

Small enough to tour in just a few hours, this seventeen-acre zoo is recognized as one of the finest small zoos in the country. Along with providing sanctuary for several endangered species, Reid Park Zoo is actively involved in breeding programs to help preserve these invaluable resources for future generations. At the same time, Reid Park Zoo is also committed to educating its visitors about the importance of conservation.

Exhibits are clearly signed, giving information about the animals, their origin, and breeding information. Docents are available to answer questions and provide information. Special events, such as the festival of lights in the winter, rain forest month, and an ice cream social, are held each year, attracting residents and visitors alike. If you're visiting the zoo with a group, make reservations ahead and enjoy the zoo with a tour guide at no charge. If you have small children, check under the veranda at the snack bar; they also rent strollers.

The zoo can only be reached by turning north into the park onto Lakeshore Lane from 22nd Street. Follow the signs to the zoo parking lot and entrance.

Tucson Botanical Gardens

If your heart is set on having a garden in Tucson, make your way to 2150 North Alvernon Way. Tucson Botanical

Gardens are an encouragement to black thumb gardeners everywhere. Formerly a private home, the Gardens are a primary source for gardening and plant information and landscaping ideas and are open seven days a week.

Visitors can attend a lecture on "Birds and Gardening" on Tuesday mornings. On Saturday mornings there's an hour-long tour of the grounds, a great way to be introduced to TBG's nooks and crannies. Or stroll around the grounds through the paths on your own tour. Numerous different gardens are scattered throughout this 5.5-acre oasis; new and exciting discoveries are around every corner. There is the Rodney Engard Cactus and Succulent Garden, established in 1991. Don't miss the sensory garden or herb garden, and check out how the tropical rain forest is coming along.

In 1988 a xeriscape garden was created to demonstrate water-thrifty gardening. Here Tucson residents new and old learn how to achieve landscaping results that are equally beautiful and water thrifty. Xeriscaping takes advantage of the adaptation that native vegetation has already made to this climate, and allows us all to benefit by conserving the desert's most precious resource, water. In the southeast corner of the Gardens, the Rodney Engard Cactus and Succulent Garden showcases many different species of cacti and related plants. There are several treats in store for you at the Dr. Scholl Foundation Sensory Garden. In addition, in 1993 Tucson Botanical Gardens grew some more by expanding its herb garden and adding a gazebo, outdoor amphitheater, and backyard bird garden.

The five-acre grounds of Tucson Botanical Gardens are home to three other organizations. Native Seeds/SEARCH is dedicated to keeping historically valuable plants from becoming extinct. Join them, by planting the same seed as Native Americans did a thousand or more years ago in your garden. Seed packets are available for purchase at the gift shop.

Growing Connections, another organization housed at TBG, showcases kitchen gardens from around the world in its multicultural garden for children. Here too is the compost demonstration site maintained by Tucson Organic Gardeners.

Twice a year, spring and fall, TBG holds a plant sale. This is a very popular event in Tucson, as is La Fiesta de los Chilis, held in October. Tucson Botanical Gardens hosts an annual Herb Fair (in May) and the Native Plant Ball, held in the summer. Many classes and workshops are held at TBG. New residents in particular may want to attend the popular Gardening in Tucson for the Newcomer, given monthly.

"A" Mountain

Southwest of downtown Tucson is a single hill. It's hard to miss, with that big fat white "A" facing the city from it. "A" Mountain was originally named Sentinel Peak. During presidio and territorial times this 3,100-foot peak was a lookout post. Advance warning of marauding Apaches could mean the difference between surviving an attack and surviving after the attack. Knowing raiders were coming not only allowed people to gather within the presidio walls, but gave them time to bring livestock safely inside as well.

After Arizona became a state, Sentinel Peak faded into the background until October 1915. Celebrating a football victory, students of the University of Arizona spent fourteen Saturdays digging a trench on the mountainside facing town. Once the trenches were complete they were filled with rocks. On the last day, classes were canceled and every student joined in. Buckets of cement were passed up a human chain to be poured out around the rocks. By nightfall its first coat of whitewash had been applied, and the big "A" was visible for miles around.

Since then, it's been a yearly tradition in the fall. On Friday night prior to the Wildcat's Homecoming football game there's a bonfire near Old Main. At the same time, members of the senior class outline the "A" with flares. The next morning as part of the homecoming and "A Day" celebration, a cavalcade of freshmen wind their way up the mountainside and apply a new coat of whitewash to the stones.

"A" Mountain also provides one of the more panoramic vantage points for viewing the city, particularly at night. To reach the overlook take Congress Street to Cuesta, turn south, and continue on Sentinel Peak Road.

Museums

Tucson is an eclectic city. It gracefully manages a rather complicated balancing act, bringing itself into the modern world while retaining much of the flavor and tradition of our varied past. Tucson's museums aid in this process by reminding us of the richness of that past, showing us the present, and opening the door on our future.

The Arizona Historical Society

The Arizona Historical Society is located at 949 East Second Street, just outside the university campus. There's a visitors' parking lot one block west, at the corner of Second and Euclid. Tokens for free parking are available at the society.

The society is Arizona's oldest cultural institution. Founded in 1884 as the Society of Arizona Pioneers, long before Arizona became a state, it was originally more a brotherhood than a historical society. A primary objective of the Pioneers was to remove "all hostile Indians . . . from the Territory at the earliest opportunity." Once that was accomplished, by 1886, the society seemed to lose steam and for nearly thirty years was not much more than a social club.

The society changed its name to the Arizona Pioneers Historical Society in 1897. By either name, the society was closed to women until the 1920s, although a woman's auxiliary was begun in 1902. (Someone had to do the work.) Ironically it was a woman, Edith Kitt, who turned the society around after becoming historical secretary in 1925.

In 1980 the society underwent another name change and became the Arizona Historical Society. Today it boasts some 4,000 members statewide. The society's museum has more than 25,000 artifacts that trace Arizona's history from before the Spanish conquest to modern times. These are displayed in both changing and permanent exhibits. The visitor is urged to visit the museum more than once to see as much as possible. Its library and reading room, open to the public at no charge, contain half a million photographic images and over 40,000 texts. The extensive archives make the society Arizona's largest historical research center.

Before entering the museum, notice the arched portal and rose-window frame in the front. Carved in 1882-1883 for the facade of the original Catedral de San Agustín, it was purchased in 1936 for seventy-five dollars by George W. Chambers when the church was condemned. When the society enlarged its museum, Mr. Chambers donated the portal to be used in the main entrance.

The society also sponsors the annual Waila Festival in the spring, showcasing the music and arts of the Tohono O'odham, and the annual Fiesta de San Agustín, held in late August. They also offer many different educational programs. These include guided tours of the museum, lectures, concerts, movie series, ranch tours, and much more. Children can learn about Arizona's rich heritage by attending Museum Discovery, a day camp offered during the summers.

Don't miss the Arizona Mining Exhibit, whatever your age. Walking through this two-story, eighty-five-foot-long, one-to-one reproduction of a copper mine as it would have appeared in operation around 1910 gives you a new perspective. Included in the display is a fully equipped blacksmith shop, a typical miner's cabin, and an assay office, and your tour is accompanied by a taped narrative of life in a mining camp. The milling setup displays machines actually used in Arizona's mining industry during 1910. These include an ore dumping car, roll crusher, jaw crusher, screen sorter, and stamp mill.

The society also has a gift shop, the Territorial Mercantile Company, and it's worth a visit all by itself. Walking into the store is like walking back into the 1870s. It's operated by the Arizona Pathfinders, an auxiliary of the society, and the volunteers wear period clothes. Here you'll find antiques, Mexican pottery, and baskets made by O'odham, Apache, and Tarahumara craftspeople.

Tucson Children's Museum

If you have young ones, take a morning or afternoon out to explore the Tucson Children's Museum. Recently moved into the historic Carnegie Library building at 200 South Sixth Avenue, it offers presentations as well as participatory programs. Its over 10,000 square feet of exhibition space is well put to use and engages young minds and old with its interesting facts and hands-on experiments.

Arizona State Museum

Contrary to its name, the Arizona State Museum is located on the University of Arizona Campus, not at ASU (Arizona State University) in Tempe. Located on University Boulevard inside the Main Gate of the U of A, it originally started life as the Territorial Museum. In 1912 when Arizona achieved statehood, it became the Arizona State Museum and has moved from its original housing inside Old Main to the South and North buildings.

Exhibits in the South Building focus on prehistory and archeology of early inhabitants, and the interrelationship of the people of the Southwest (particularly Arizona) and the area's natural history and environment. Because artifacts from many different Native American cultures are exhibited, visitors can learn to distinguish the work of one tribe from another. The gift shop in the South Building also contains craft work from local artisans, including Navajo, Pueblo, Hopi, O'odham, Tarahumara, and Pima. The selection offers rugs, pottery, baskets, and jewelry as well as books about the area.

The North Building houses the newest exhibits, featuring ten Southwestern tribes. What is unique about this is that each exhibit uses an internal perspective, viewing themselves from within. This uncommon focus provides visitors with a more human appreciation of the people who made this land their home long before Europeans began their westward journey.

Titan Missile Museum

Some of Tucson's past is very modern. As befits a frontier town, Tucsonans have been in the forefront of the air and space industry since its inception. The Titan Missile Museum is a chilling reminder of just how much so. The museum is an actual deactivated Titan II missile site, one of the eighteen which were located in the Tucson area. For nearly twenty years Air Force crews spent long hours in this silo, waiting for the call that luckily never came.

Pursuant to agreements between the U.S. Air Force, local officials, SAC, DOD, and the (then) Soviets, today the missile site is open to the public. Beginning with a short film, visitors proceed down (and up) a fifty-five-step stairway (low heels are advised) into the silo itself. The elaborate controls in the command center and the awesome size of the missile (still in the silo, sans booster and warhead), coupled with memories of "duck and cover" drills, are worth the effort. You can look down at the missile itself through the glass covering the partially open silo doors. There's also a small gift shop on the premises.

Pima Air and Space Museum

Close to Davis Monthan AFB at 6000 East Valencia, the Pima Air and Space Museum is housed in a 20,000-square-foot building that provides ample room for its exhibits, which include several aircraft suspended from the ceiling. Both aircraft artifacts and memorabilia are on display inside, and outside are some 180 vintage and historic aircraft. This is the world's largest private collection of historic aircraft, including a Boeing B-29 "Superfortress" and a North American F-100C "Supersabre," the first jet fighter to exceed the speed of sound in level flight. Visitors can even tour Air Force One. Not the current airplane, of course, this is the plane that was used by Presidents Kennedy and Johnson. The tour is given every half-hour or so and is open to any museum visitor.

There's a gift shop with an abundance of models, publications, and other items all centered around aircraft. One word of caution: Before touring the planes outside, consider the time of day (and year). A good pair of walking shoes is recommended at any time, as is sunscreen and a hat.

Fort Lowell Museum

Located in Fort Lowell Park at Craycroft and Glenn, the Fort Lowell Museum is not your everyday museum. While there are two buildings to tour, instead of wide arching halls and display cases the majority of the museum is outside, on the grounds of Fort Lowell Park. The museum building reconstructs the quarters of the fort's commanding officer circa 1886, and includes photographs, maps, uniforms, and equipment of the time. The second building, once the CO's kitchen, adds archeological exhibits and a photographic exhibit of Arizona history.

The original Fort Lowell was a temporary post, established in 1866 and located inside the Old Presidio, roughly where the Santa Rita Hotel is today. Whether it was the town corrupting the men, or the men stationed there corrupting Tucson, in 1873 it was decided to move the post seven miles northeast near the banks of Rillito Creek, today a deeply cut and usually dry bed but then flowing year round with water. This was not considered a pleasant posting in those days. Bitter complaints rose from the men over the terrific windstorms they had to endure, and the distance supplies had to come from town. (Seven miles isn't what it used to be, obviously.) Eventually more storage facilities were built, and then a hospital, barracks, and officers' quarters rose from the sandy ground.

Designated a fort in 1879, then becoming Regional HQ for the Fifth U.S. Calvary, eventually Fort Lowell's reputation grew until a posting there was welcomed. Walter Reed served a year's posting as surgeon at the fort hospital. The fort supplied outlying forts nearer Apache country, and during the Apache wars held its share of troops brought into the area.

It wasn't all grim duty, however. Social events engaging both Tucson citizens and men stationed at the fort were many, both at the fort and in town. The Fifth Cavalry Band was on hand for military balls as well as concerts in Tucson parks, while dinners, dances, and receptions rounded out their social life.

After Geronimo's capture in 1886 and subsequent diminishment of the Apache menace, much of the reason for maintaining the fort disappeared. In 1891 the fort was ordered closed, and the troops were sent north to the plains after marauding Sioux tribesmen. Today, only crumbling ruins remain of the sturdy adobe fort walls. Stands throughout the park help visitors orient themselves to the surviving structures, overlaying present-day images with the ghosts of Tucson's past.

Tucson's very far past, in fact. Near the center rear of the park is the Hardy site, with remains of a Hohokam village. The signs around the site help the visitor understand what their daily routine must have been like when the

Rillito was a meandering stream, not a deeply cut occasional waterway through the desert. If you'd like to see what the area must have been like then, at the eastern edge of the park is a stream fed by a recirculating pump. Here you can see what a desert riparian area is like close up.

Of course, Fort Lowell the park isn't totally focused on the past. Bring a lunch and enjoy the shade of the eucalyptus and cottonwood trees. The view of the Catalinas isn't too shabby, either. Bring a bat and ball, and hit a few from one of the baseball diamonds. If there's a soccer player in the group, Fort Lowell is one of the sites for the Shoot-Out, national soccer playoffs held annually in Tucson. The park also offers swimming, a duck pond, walking routes, and racquetball and tennis courts.

Artes de Tucson

Almost everyone has heard of Tucson's Ted De Grazia. His work helped popularize Southwest images in the art world. However, he isn't Tucson's only artistic claim to fame. Only fourteen cities in the entire United States have a full complement of the performing arts. This sleepy little ol' cow town surprises visitors when they learn that Tucson is one of this elite circle. With its own symphony, theater, ballet, and opera companies, each operating independently of each other, the aficionado of the arts is certain to find a full palette in Tucson from which to choose.

For many years the University of Arizona was Tucson's cultural center, so it seems fit to begin there. Every year students of the university put on a number of very professional theatrical productions. These are presented either at the Peter Marroney Theater, which is near Park and Speedway on campus, or at the Repertory Theater, behind the Marroney Theater.

Visiting professional artists can be seen and heard at Centennial Hall, as part of the University of Arizona Artist Series. Top quality talent is a standard here, featuring such names as Ladysmith Black Mambazo, Teatro de Danza Española, Judy Collins, and Tony Bennett.

Pima Community College has artistic leanings, as well. Both plays and concerts are presented at the Pima Community College District Center for the Arts.

Tucson Symphony Orchestra

If good music attracts you, there are a number of off-campus choices as well. For sixty-six years the Tucson Symphony Orchestra has offered concerts both in the concert hall and at guest sites throughout the city. Sometimes these music fests are held under a roof, sometimes outside under the stars at a local park. Frequently guest artists are featured.

Arizona Opera

For those more vocally inclined when it comes to music, there are two choices. Purists may prefer the Arizona Opera, presenting classical favorites from Wagner, Bizet, and others. For a lighter touch check out the Southern Arizona Light Opera Company. Notice that's "Light" Opera. Their 1995 productions included *Guys and Dolls* and *Cinderella* (yes, in English). A screen showing an English translation of operas written in another language is helpful to many.

Arizona Theatre Company

Plays are also put on by the Arizona Theatre Company, ranging from comedy to drama to musicals. Held at the Temple of Music and Art, many feature well-known directors and actors as well as locals.

Arizona Ballet

Dance is also well represented in Tucson, not least by the Arizona Ballet. Their yearly presentation of the *Nutcracker* at Christmas time features local students in the role of Clara and other children. The rest of the year concentrates on classical ballet productions, such as *Swan Lake* and *Cinderella*.

Private operations such as The Gaslight Theatre and The Invisible Theatre add to Tucson's local art scene. These theaters provide a public outlet for original work and new artists, both writers and actors, while giving residents and visitors alike an opportunity to see new productions.

Galleries

Tucson is a city of artists, but if you can't see their work it's hard to appreciate them. Fortunately, Tucson has a number of exciting galleries. While the De Grazia Gallery concentrates, not surprisingly, on the work of Ted De Grazia, it also exhibits work of other artists in changing shows. Other galleries are even more eclectic, with constantly changing exhibits featuring both local and national artists in many mediums.

One of many interesting places is the Philabaum Studio. Both a working artist's studio and an art gallery, what makes it truly unusual is that the medium in question is glass. There's a window between the work being done and the viewer, so you're also spared some of the heat. Watching these works evolve from what seems almost a liquid substance is quite an extraordinary experience.

For a complete listing of who is showing what where, as well as lucid comments on the content of the shows, we again refer you to the *Tucson Weekly* newspaper, the *Tucson Official Visitors Guide*, or the *Tucson Guide Quarterly*. Or plan to be downtown the first Saturday of some month. That's when Downtown Saturday Night concentrates on the arts district, and the galleries and studios are open to the public, showing off their best pretties.

Many Tucson museums also function as galleries, with both permanent and changing exhibits. These may feature items that are part of their permanent collection, or the work of visiting artists. Chief among these are the Tucson Museum of Art and the John P. Schaefer Center for Creative Photography.

De Grazia Gallery in the Sun

When Ettore "Ted" De Grazia began building at the end of North Swan Road, his future studio was w-a-a-y out in the boonies. Now the De Grazia Gallery in the Sun is part of the Catalina foothills, part of the city. The first building that went up at De Grazia's hands was the Mission in the Sun, a chapel dedicated to Nuestra Senora de Guadalupe (Our Lady of Guadalupe), patron saint of Mexico.

The gallery is his design and displays many of his original works, paintings, bronzes, and enamels in both permanent and rotating exhibits. If you'd like to know more about De Grazia as an artist, the University of Arizona produced a twenty-five-minute film on the subject. You can view it at the gallery in the movie room; just ask any of the staff and they'll start the show. There are also books on his life and work in the gift shop, as well as a variety of other items from prints to collectibles. A smaller companion gallery exhibits the works of visiting artists.

Even non-artists still fondly remember his "tax revolt" in the 1970s. He was disgusted with the IRS and its inheritance tax rulings as they affected the worth of his paintings. Armed with a bottle of Chivas Regal, he took a great stack of his paintings, doused them with the Chivas, and set them afire.

It was shortly thereafter that the De Grazia Art and Cultural Foundation was created. The foundation has operated the De Grazia Gallery in the Sun since De Grazia's death in 1982. The gallery features his work and allows visitors to trace the development and maturation of his artistic style over the years.

Shopping

Now we ask you—where would a self-respecting tourist town be without shopping opportunities? In addition to the major malls that are typical for most cities, Tucson has a number of gallerias and small shopping centers that provide a mixture of Southwest and modern for the sophisticated shopper

Tucson Mall

Of the four major malls in the Tucson area, the newest and largest is the Tucson Mall. It is located north of downtown at 4500 North Oracle Road. It has over 200 shops anchored by Dillard's, Foley's, JCPenny, Mervyn's, Sears, and The Broadway, and it features a collection of Southwestern specialty shops called *Arizona Avenue.*

El Con Mall

El Con Mall is Tucson's mid-town mall, located on Broadway west of Alvernon. It takes its name from the El Conquistador Resort, which occupied the same land during the 1930s. Today all that remains of the resort is their water tower across the street (see page 150). The El Con has over 140 stores and restaurants and is anchored by Foley's, Dilllard's, JCPenney, and Montgomery Ward.

Park Mall

Park Mall, at 5870 E. Broadway, serves the city's east side. This mall was once on the outskirts of town. Where the mall is now was native desert. Now residents are buffered (somewhat) from the mall traffic and lights by a tall brick wall and strip park, and the outskirts of town have been pushed back quite a bit. The Park Mall features over 120 stores and is anchored by Dillard's, Sears, and The Broadway.

Foothills Mall

Foothills Mall on La Cholla at Ina Road is the northwest side of the city's mall. It's a more modest mall and features small boutiques specializing in Southwestern items. It has been undergoing some major changes and now features a Barnes and Noble Super Store.

Fourth Avenue

Another different type of shopping area—definitely not a mall—is Fourth Avenue, specifically that portion of Fourth Avenue between University and Ninth Street. The trolley runs up and down this area, and an all-day pass is only $2.50. It's a mellange of shops, many women-owned and women-oriented. These include the self-proclaimed feminist Antigone Bookstore and Mystic Moon. While both feature products (books to bumper stickers) that empower women, Mystic Moon welcomes Wiccans and offers botanical items.

The clothes on Fourth Avenue aren't like those anywhere else. If you enjoy "retro-chic," stop in at How Sweet It Was. The Jewel Thief offers fashionably funky clothes and is a favorite of U of A students. The career woman's choice, Jasmine specializes in sophisticated, singular styles. Creations, another clothing store, focuses on lovely, filmy, slinky attire.

Many of the clothing stores offer imported accessories, jewelry, and bags, but Del Sol is a one-stop cornucopia. An outlet for reservation traders, here you can find everything from Native American rugs, basketry, and pottery to hand-woven Guatemalan fashions.

Fourth Avenue offers food for the inner wo/man, as well. You can choose between ethnic, organic, and health-conscious restaurants, or grab a slice of pizza. Natural cooks will enjoy shopping at the Food Conspiracy Co-op, which offers organic produce and other products, some of which are grown locally. If you start to tire out halfway down the Avenue, the Epic Cafe is a great place to rest and people-watch. It's a coffeehouse that offers food and encourages you to take your time. And for dessert, don't overlook the Chocolate Iguana.

The best introduction you can have to Fourth Avenue is the Fourth Avenue Fair. See that under Craft Fairs, below.

Western Shops

If you can't find Western clothes in Tucson, you haven't looked. Arizona Hatters, Arizona Outfitters Western Wear, Corral Western Wear, Stewart Boot Manufacturers, Western Warehouse, and the many specialty shops in the malls will provide all the choices you want.

Neighborhood Centers

Would you rather shop in relative quiet, not facing the crowds at the malls? Tucson's neighborhood centers offer an excellent selection. El Mercado, The River Center, Santa Fe Square, St. Phillip's Plaza Merchants, and others offer many interesting shops.

Old Town Artisans

Old Town Artisans, located downtown at 186 North Meyer Avenue, is another non-mall collection of small shops, but the focus in this square block is on fine quality handwork. Over 150 local craft workers pursue their trade here, housed by renovated adobe buildings dating from antebellum days. Look up when you go inside; the saguaro rib ceilings are original.

Any number of different craft disciplines are represented here, including many American Indian as well as Latin selections. Jewelry, pottery, one-of-a-kind fashions—whether you're looking for something for yourself or a gift, there's a fine variety to choose from. There's also the Courtyard Cafe with its fine patio for the pause that refreshes. Old Town Artisans is part of the El Presidio Historic District. It's been undergoing restoration since 1978, housing artist's studios and galleries as a way of nurturing the growth of the arts in Tucson.

The Lost Barrio

When Tucson was barely past village stage, around the turn of the century, South Park Avenue used to be the theater district. Then warehouses were built in 1908. Today, the warehouses are filled with some of the most unique shops (and a gallery) in the Tucson area. Called by some the Lost Barrio Warehouses and by others SoBro (South of Broadway), they stretch along South Park between Twelfth and Manlove streets.

The area got its first shop in 1987 when Rústica moved into Number 200. Now there are two furniture and interior design shops. There are also two art galleries, a Mexican restaurant, an import store, and a shop doing custom Roman shades and iron work, all with a distinctive Southwestern flavor. Drive by—you're there when you see their brightly painted doors against the old red warehouse bricks.

The Fourth Avenue Street Fair

The Fourth Avenue Street Fair celebrated its twenty-sixth anniversary in 1996, and it was a glorious success. Now held twice a year (December and again in March or April), during the fair Fourth Avenue is closed off and vendors' booths line up back-to-back down the middle of the avenue from University to Ninth Street. What with the tie-dyed clothes, ethnic music, and street jugglers, the Fourth Avenue Street Fair is a time trip back to the '60s. There's no admission fee; just walk inside the barricades and meander down the avenue.

Because the over 300 vendor booths set up back-to-back, you have to go all the way down, and then turn around and come back up the other side in order to see them all. This allows you to window-shop the stores along the way as well. From quality gemstones to "spoon" jewelry, bread-dough figures to fine art, dream-catchers and train whistles, it's all here somewhere. If it's not in a booth, it's probably in one of the stores and restaurants along the avenue.

Craft Fairs

Fort Lowell Park hosts a major arts and crafts fair twice a year, in March and October. The emphasis here is on hand-made items; from scrimshaw work to train whistles, crafts-people congregate here from all over the country. Both fairs at Fort Lowell Park also have a goodly assortment of antiques, again attracting dealers and collectors nationwide.

Reid Park also hosts arts and crafts fairs four times a year. Its November event is the perfect place to find unique Christmas gifts. Both local and nationally known craft workers display during these affairs.

Check the *Official Visitors Guide* or the *Tucson Guide Quarterly* for listings of the many arts and craft fairs that happen over the course of the year.

Tucson Gem and Mineral Show

For over forty years, every February has seen the Tucson Gem and Mineral Show arrive in Tucson. A huge production, dealers and buyers from every state and over forty different countries around the world visit Tucson every February to display, sell, buy, and admire minerals, fossils, and gemstones. Held at the Tucson Convention Center, practically every room in Tucson is sold out for the duration, sometimes reserved a year in advance immediately following the previous year's show.

While many of the "dealer rooms" are closed to all but dealers, the main show at the Tucson Convention Center welcomes the public. Packed with exhibits and dealers, every year a different mineral is chosen as the show's theme. This is a terrific learning experience for any age, with lectures and educational presentations. The Tucson Convention Center is divided down the middle by display cases holding extraordinary displays of gemstones and jewelry. Whether you buy something or not, with selections ranging in price from pennies to thousands of dollars, the show is well worth at least one afternoon.

Artisans Market

The Tucson Museum of Art sponsors a yearly Artisans Market that draws some of the best craft workers and artisans in the Southwest to Tucson. While Tucson has a number of craft and antique fairs during the year, the items featured at the Artisans Market are closer to fine arts (and some, but not all, are priced accordingly).

Thrifty Tucson

There are used bookstores just about everywhere. We know that. So why mention a used bookstore in a book about Tucson? Because Bookman's has back copies of *Arizona Highways*. Boxes of them! *Arizona Highways*, published by the Arizona Department of Transportation, is filled with outstanding photographs. This prizewinning magazine has probably introduced Arizona to more people in the world than any other single source. If the publication is new to you, this is a wonderful way to introduce yourself. Known for its unparalleled photographs of desert beauty, *Arizona Highways* is highly prized by many whether they've visited Arizona or not.

Of course, Bookman's has more than just back copies of *AH*. They sell (and buy) both used and new books and magazines, as well as used records, video games, CD's, videos, and computer software. They also take requests, so if something you're looking for comes in, they notify you and hold it for you. And with two locations, there are hours of browsing ahead.

Someone once said that Tucson was the second-hand capital of the Southwest. You'll find a number of shops like Buffalo Exchange or Not Just Plain Jane's that will help spread your clothing budget without embarrassment.

Don't limit your shopping expereince. Consult the Tucson *Official Visitor Guide* and the *Tucson Guide Quarterly* for a complete list of shops, and even swap meets (the Tanque Verde Swap Meet has a twenty-year history), more than enough to fill those hours when only shopping can satisfy.

Casinos

The northern border of the mile-square Pasqua Yaqui Indian Reservation runs along the south side of Valencia Road, west of I-19. You can tempt Lady Luck here in their Casino of the Sun. Originally a 1,000-seat bingo hall, it was expanded in 1995 into a complete casino. The remodeling job didn't replace bingo, however. It grew into the Bingodome. You can even play MegaBingo, a televised bingo game linked to other states, with jackpots occasionally reaching a million dollars.

The Tohono O'dham Indian Reservation also has a casino, the Desert Diamond Casino. It is located east of I-19 on Old Nogales Highway, just south of Valencia Road.

Both casinos offer Las Vegas style gambling. There's live keno, slot machines and video poker, and keno machines. If you prefer cards, take a chair at one of the tables in the card room and try your luck. The tables offer seven-card stud, pai gow, Texas hold'em, Omaha, and Arizona 21 (the house variety of blackjack).

Transportation to and from either casino is available by calling toll-free numbers. These casinos have rapidly become a vital resource for the tribes, funding tribal programs from education to health services. Profits from the casinos will also be used in new business ventures for the tribes.

Dude Ranches

The ranch house of the Flying V Ranch was built in 1907. Catering to the more sedate nature-lover, its sixty-nine acres are located at the mouth of Ventana Canyon. This area along Ventana Creek in the Catalina Mountains is a hiker's (or bird-lover's) paradise. It has been operated as a guest house since 1942, with five rock and stucco cottages available for guests. It has its own pool and is right next door to Loews Ventana Canyon Resort (which has everything; see page 176).

White Stallion Ranch has been around for thirty years as a family-owned and operated guest ranch, seventeen miles northwest of Tucson. When the Towne's bought the place in 1958, they wanted to name it after their favorite horse story, *The Black Stallion*. Somehow, though, the initials BS just didn't seem to fit the image they wanted to project as a guest ranch, so the horse changed color.

Now owned by the True family, it is the largest facility in the area with 3,000 acres of its own. More than that, as far as trails go, because it's located right next to Saguaro National Park-West. Its family orientation is reflected in its high return rate, offering accommodations for seventy-five people in twenty-nine guest rooms.

There's a weekly rodeo featuring team roping, steer wrestling, and horse cutting for guests, and horseback riding is a favorite activity. They offer four rides a day, two fast and two slow. The slower rides are a perfect introduction to the experience, and children five years and over are welcomed.

The Lazy K Bar Guest Ranch has been in operation for fifty years and under the same ownership for the last twenty; they've learned a few things about treating their guests right. Just sixteen miles northwest of Tucson, located at the base of Safford Peak in the Tucson Mountains, it's also right next to Saguaro National Park-West, which add substantially to the number of available riding and hiking trails. You can follow one of their guided horseback rides with a soak in the Jacuzzi, attend the cookout, then choose between the hayride or western dancing. If you enjoy shooting, ask about the possibilities of scaring up a few skeet.

Excursions to Old Tucson or the Arizona-Sonora Desert Museum are offered on Sundays. Their twenty rooms share one outstanding feature: no telephone or television! Don't panic, there's a huge screen in the TV room so addicts can stave off withdrawal. On Saturdays there's a steak cookout, and you won't believe the waterfall! (Bar facilities are provided at the Longhorn Bar, strictly BYOB.)

The Tanque Verde Guest Ranch was originally named La Cebadilla for the wild barley that grows along the banks of the Tanque Verde Creek. The ranch is nestled into the foothills of the Rincon Mountains. To get there go all the way out East Speedway until the road dead-ends at the trail head into the Rincons. Turn left instead, and follow the road to the ranch. (The ranch also operates a shuttle for guests.) Dating back to a land grant, Tanque Verde continues as a working cattle ranch, but that operation is at a different site from the guest ranch. The background gives a rustic authenticity to the accommodations, but in all other respects it lives up to its Mobile Four-Star rating.

In addition to guided hikes and horseback rides through the Rincons, a naturalist is on staff, available to answer guests' questions as well as give nature talks and presentations. For those who want a vacation away from the kids but have the kids along, the children's program allows just that. Kids from four to eleven can spend nearly the entire day with a counselor (yes, evening too) with riding lessons, fishing, and other activities. Major pleasant surprise— there's no additional charge if you decide to take advantage of this option.

If you plan to see more of the area, there are sightseeing trips to locations all around the valley, including shopping trips into Mexico. Although there's no golf course on the ranch, Tanque Verde guests do have privileges at six Tucson courses and clubs. The El Sonora Spa is a complete indoor facility from swimming pool to exercise room.

Resorts

There isn't room to cover all the possibilities here, but a few of the most outstanding and best known include Loews Ventana Canyon Resort, Westin La Paloma, Canyon Ranch Health and Fitness Resort, and the Tucson National Golf & Conference Resort.

Perhaps the best thing about Loews Ventana Canyon Resort is that you don't have to be staying there to use the facilities. Those who are guests have a private terrace to enjoy the wonderful view. Snuggled up against Ventana Canyon, their two private 18-hole golf courses, designed by Tom Fazio, are PGA rated. After golf or tennis, choose between the spa, Jacuzzi, sauna, or steam room before making the harder choice between their five restaurants and lounges.

Westin La Paloma is Tucson's largest hotel in terms of capacity, and features a Jack Nicklaus signature golf course of 27 holes. And with five restaurants to choose from, you may need to visit their on-site health center just to keep pace.

Canyon Ranch Health and Fitness Resort concentrates on offering the ultimate spa experience. Guests can enjoy early morning walks, fitness classes, consultations, and workshops in beautiful surroundings, inside and out. Concentrate on healthy living through nutritional and fitness counseling, have a private sports lesson, or opt for a total body experience in their spa.

Tucson National Golf & Conference Resort terms itself a "boutique" resort. Home of the Northern Telecom Open, a PGA tour event, it offers 27 holes of championship golf on their semiprivate course. The facility also has tennis courts, a pool (of course), and a luxurious European-style spa to get you in shape for dinner at their Fiesta Dining Room.

Touring from Tucson

Whether you live in Tucson or are just here for a visit, try to make sure you have time to visit some of the interesting places in our general area. You'll find that being in the desert tended to group people together, with nothing but a lot of open desert in between. Tucson was the hub for them then, as it still is now.

Madera Canyon

Madera Canyon is in the Santa Rita Mountains, about a forty-minute drive down I-19. Year-round hiking is one of the attractions. When snow covers high northern slopes, the southern approaches and trails beckon. With some eighty-five named canyons, many with streams fed either by runoff or springs, and fifty-two summits, of which twenty-nine are over 6,000 feet, there's enough variety for a lifetime of exploration.

There are trails to almost all the peaks, which some say can be quite grueling. If you are an avid and experienced hiker, you may want to check them out. A popular route is the trail to Old Baldy, highest peak in the range, which rises 4,000 feet through its 5.4-mile route. Most trails begin at elevations between 4,000 and 5,500 feet. Many trails begin from Madera Canyon, but by no means all. For a comprehensive hiking guide specific for the Santa Ritas, see Bob and Dotty Martin's *Hiking Guide to the Santa Rita Mountains of Arizona.*

Madera Canyon is nestled into the northern face of the Santa Ritas. At 5,000 feet of elevation, it averages about 15 degrees cooler than Tucson and is a popular refuge from Tucson's summer heat. Of course, you don't have to wait for summer. Madera Canyon is beautiful any time of the year. To reach the canyon, take I-19 to Green Valley, then 98 to the Madera Turnoff. While the road leads into the mountains, it's a gentle climb.

For a marvelous introduction to the delights of Madera Canyon, continue driving until you arrive at the Santa Rita Lodge. There are parking sites in front of the lodge; if there's an open space, take it. The front lawn of the lodge is large and dotted with trees. Find a place to sit, and enjoy the show.

Each tree on the lawn has multiple hummingbird feeders hanging from it. And are they popular! In this one spot you may see more different varieties of hummingbirds than you knew existed. And this is just the appetizer.

Since Madera Canyon is partially riparian and fully protected, many varieties of birds, animals, and lizards can be seen. Further down the road past the lodge are more parking sites, and then the road ends. Trails abound through the area; just remember to take the binoculars when you leave the car. During the summer up to 200 species of birds can be found here, including the elegant trogon. This colorful yellow-billed bird has lured many a birdwatcher to Madera Canyon in hopes of catching a glimpse. Also called the coppery-tailed trogon, the male has a glossy green head and chest with a bright red belly, the green and red being separated by a white strip across its chest. The female has a brown head and chest instead of green, a much wider pale band across her chest, and a white cheek mark the male lacks.

A number of other animals also live in this wildlife refuge, from deer to puma, coyote to fox, bobcats and black bears. Remember that this is their home, and you're just visiting.

There are nearly one hundred miles of hiking trails leaving from Madera Canyon area into the Santa Ritas. You can picnic or camp out at Bog Springs (for a fee), or stay at the Santa Rita Lodge to enjoy the area for a longer time. The lodge offers both rooms and cabins, all equipped with kitchenettes. This is a popular place, particularly with bird watchers. Reservations are suggested, particularly in the busy summer season.

Tubac, Tumacacori, and Nogales

What used to be at least a day or two or three's hard distance is now only a couple of hours away by car, a good way to spend a Saturday. Within a reasonable driving distance of Tucson are three good destinations: Tubac, Tumacacori, and Nogales. If you want to make all three places the same day, better start early in the day. You may want to make two trips out of it, depending on your interests. If you're of the disposition to spend a lot of time shopping, you might want to spend more time at Tubac. If so, you might consider taking another day to head directly to Nogales. Tumacacori is another of the missions Fr. Kino established, but not quite in the same shape as San Xavier. These are interesting places that can give you a better idea of what it was like to live in the Southwest desert.

South of Tucson the freeway I-10 takes a turn to the east, while the I-19 freeway continues to head almost directly south. Take the latter to travel to Mexico. It leads down through what once was known as the Dead Man's Highway, because so many people were buried along it. The Indians and robbers killed anybody found traveling it.

Today, however, it is a pleasant drive down an uncrowded freeway. Just to keep you on your lookout, this highway is marked in kilometers, not miles. A kilometer is just a little over a half-mile long (0.621 to be exact).

Tubac

Some ten or fifteen miles past San Xavier Mission and the end of the reservation is Green Valley, one of Arizona's original retirement communities. The huge plateaus you see on the west side of the road opposite Green Valley aren't natural, incidentally. Those are tailings (rock and gravel discarded after ore extraction) from the open pit copper mine further west. You can get a small idea of its size from what's been piled up.

About twenty-five miles further south you encounter Tubac. This is a dual stop, combining history with art. The Presidio de San Ignacio de Tubac was founded here June 1752, the year after the Pima revolt. It was located on the banks of the Santa Cruz River and was built to protect both settlers and area missions.

Juan Bautista de Anza was the second commander of the presidio. In 1774 he and Fray Francisco Garcés (cofounder of Tucson) left Tubac with a group of colonists to search for an overland route to California. Garcés stopped at Yuma, but de Anza continued on, and the colonists he led became the founders of the city of San Francisco. In 1776 the presidio and its men were moved to Tucson, leaving the area

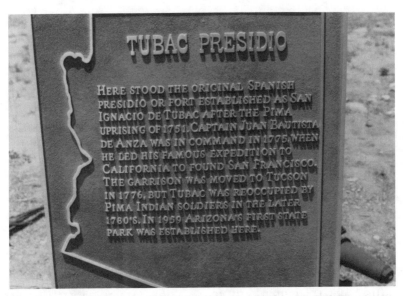

The Tubac Presidio.

vulnerable to attacks from raiding Apaches. Stubbornly, the settlers refused to move, and in 1787 another garrison, composed of Pimas commanded by Spanish officers, returned to Tubac. Apache raids increased, however, until 1830 when Tubac was again abandoned.

Following the Gadsen Purchase of 1853, Charles D. Poston arrived in the area and set up shop at Tubac, developing the nearby Heintzelman mine. When his operation was shut down by the Civil War, Tubac continued as a farming area, continuing to endure Apache raids until they finally diminished around 1890. In total, the town was abandoned eight times.

In 1948 new life came to the area when an artist's school opened. Through the years the word spread, and as more artists moved to the area it became an artists' colony. Today the Tubac Center of the Arts is thriving, with over fifty studios and galleries to explore. Spring offers the best opportunities for taking in a little of everything. In February the Tubac Festival of the Arts is held, and in March is the

Tubac Art Walk. During the Art Walk the public is invited into the artists' studios for demonstrations of their work. Both festivals draw visitors from around the world. De Anza Days in October celebrate the explorer's founding of Tubac and subsequent expedition to perform the same favor for San Francisco. In December, Christmas is celebrated with Fiesta Navidad, featuring luminarias (paper bags with candles inside) and caroling.

If you'd rather explore the area's history, visit the archaeological dig in progress. There's a lot to discover, when you consider the area was occupied by the Hohokam as early as A.D. 30. If you're lucky, you may be able to make it a hands-on experience.

Tumacacori

Continuing on south down Highway I-19, about three miles south of Tubac is Tumacacori National Historical Park. It is the site of one of the missions established by Fr. Kino in the late 1600s. This one was not as fortunate as San Xavier.

There were actually three missions founded in the area. Fr. Kino, a Jesuit, founded two of them, Tumacacori and Guevavi (which was originally the larger of the two), and the third, Calabazas, was started six years later, after the Franciscan missionaries replaced the expelled Jesuits.

Fr. Kino built the missions here because there was a large settlement of Pima Indians. The original missions were probably houses similar in construction to the ones in which the Indians lived. During the first years the missions were on the east side of the Santa Cruz. When they moved to the west of the river, after the Pima rebellion in 1751, it was decided to build a large mission structure. Construction didn't actually begin until 1879.

What remains of the mission at Tumacacori.

The fact that the missions were eventually abandoned indicates the difficult times people had living here. Surveys and explorations reveal that it was once a thriving community. The Santa Cruz provided a good location; it was the people who couldn't get along. Spanish politics forced the Jesuits out of the missionary business and replaced them with Franciscan missionaries. It was the Franciscan priests who built the mission church we now see here. The Mexicans who recovered their independence from Spain; diseases that ravaged Mexicans, Europeans, and Indians alike; war with the United States; and especially raiding Apaches, all had their effects.

These contributing factors all made it necessary to combine the three missions at Tumacacori. The shell of the church was begun in about 1800 but was never finished. The site was abandoned in 1848 after a terrible winter which was punctuated with raiding Indians.

The area had turned from one that held promises of life to one that just wasn't worth living in. The people left and with them the reasons for the church. The shell that still stands gives you some insight into their lives.

Stop off here for a pleasant visit to see what remains. It's a self-guided tour, meaning you're free to wander around and see the mission and different displays. The mission church is a large structure that was supposed to be the rival of San Xavier del Bac. Its thick adobe walls, large, three-story bell tower, and baptistery are visible as are the usual mission features.

President Theodore Roosevelt established Tumacacori National Monument in 1908, and the National Park Service took over its management in 1916. In 1980 all three missions were combined, and the name was changed to Tumacacori National Historic Park.

Nogales

You arrive in Nogales after a comfortable drive, about an hour and a half south of Tucson (not counting stops). There are two cities named Nogales. One is Nogales, Arizona, USA, the other is Nogales, Sonora, Mexico. Your destination is the Mexican city.

American citizens do not need passports or visas to spend the day there. (If you plan to stay there longer, do some research to find out what current regulations are. The Mexican Consulate is in Tucson.) You can drive your car into Mexico, but unless you're absolutely sure about your automobile insurance and international laws and regulations, it's better to park at one of the convenient places in Nogales, Arizona and walk across the border. The streets are narrow and crowded, and parking is doubtful. It's only an extra five minutes or so to park on the U.S. side and walk across, and you'll be walking around across the border anyway. Taxis are plentiful (and cheap), whether heading into town or back to the border. (If you intend to travel into Mexico, see Traveling in Mexico, page 186, for some tips.)

Of course, the real reason you go to Nogales is to shop and to see what Mexico is like. First of all, expect to find something different and to have some fun. Nogales is a border city, not necessarily indicative of what life is like in other cities in Mexico. Also be aware that, while many of the shopkeepers may appear to be uneducated, backward, and uncertain, they are experienced merchants and experts at negotiating the sale of their products.

This doesn't mean you won't find bargains. You'll find all kinds of trinkets, rugs, shawls, blankets, dresses, toys, furniture, wall hangings, glassware, leather goods, and—of course—bottled alcoholic beverages.

In general, prices for liquor in Mexico are cheaper than in the United States, but check U.S. prices before you go. Kaluha will usually be a bargain, and you may find significantly better prices for others liquors as well, notably tequila.

U.S. cash is good anywhere, and credit cards are accepted at most shops. Prices may be in dollars or pesos. When you ask a price and the clerk pulls out a calculator, s/he isn't figuring out how much to overcharge you, she's multiplying the peso price by the day's exchange rate. Yes, prices can change daily. Mexico has a very fast moving economy. Most people speak English, so even if it appears you have encountered a shopkeeper who doesn't understand English, he or she probably does.

Many tourist shops are not built to what you might consider American standards. (You're not in America—try to keep it in mind.) Many are open air, few are air conditioned, and amenities are few. Some shops have gathered together in a mall-type atmosphere, others are small shops, some are sidewalk vendors. You will also find modern stores, with expensive items.

Food and drink in Mexico is also something to be considered. If you're going to be walking around all day, you'll want some refreshment. You'll find a wide assortment of sidewalk vendors, open-air markets, and restaurants small and large. Some people like to experiment, others stick to the better restaurants and bottled drinks. A day trip to Nogales isn't worth picking up an intestinal bug.

An item that has become very popular for shopping in Nogales is prescription medicine. Prices are usually very good compared to what you pay in the United States. Some people imply the quality may be sub-par, others say that isn't so. You can make some good purchases there, but if you purchase prescription medicine without a proper prescription with you, the medicine can be confiscated at the border and a fine levied as well.

Each American citizen, even a baby, is allowed to bring in $400 worth of merchandise duty free. The purchases can be combined under one allowance so that a family of four can bring in $1,600 of purchases from perfume to jewelry without paying duty.

A shopping trip to Nogales can be a lot of fun. Approach it with the spirit of adventure and experimentation. Sample the life across the border, and don't be too surprised at what you see there. It's different, after all, and you can bring back gifts for others as well as items for yourself and family that are useful and colorful—good reminders of your visit.

Traveling in Mexico

Travel in Mexico has changed consistently and considerably in recent years. If you are traveling within the free trade zone, including the Baja California Peninsula and the Sonora free trade zone (twenty-two miles into Mexico), there are no procedures to worry about. But always carry proof of citizenship, like a driver's license.

If you travel farther into Mexico or if you're going to be there longer than seventy-two hours, you need a tourist permit. They are available at the border when you present your passport, birth certificate, and driver's license or state identification card. Make sure you are up on your legalities. Don't forget, you have to get back.

If you intend to drive, Mexican automobile insurance is usually recommended. Many U.S. insurance companies include coverage into Mexico, some don't. Be sure that the Mexican policeman who comes upon an accident scene won't know if your company has coverage or not. You and/or your car could be detained.

Taking a car beyond the free trade zone requires a procedure to go through and requirements that must be met. You also have to turn in your car permit at the 22-kilometer checkpoint. If the permit isn't in Mexico when it expires, the Mexican government likes to fine people heavily.

Make sure you contact your automobile insurance company and the Mexican consulate in Tucson before you get to Nogales.

Patagonia Lake

In the 1960s a dam was built, about seventy miles southeast from Tucson, that backed up enough water to be called a lake. Patagonia Lake, to be exact. Only a small portion of the lake is landlubber-friendly, open to the driver or walker. Much of the shoreline is accessible only by boat. The lake is small enough to explore with a rowboat, yet large enough to permit power-boaters room. Hikers can use the campground as a base, since there's trail access to the Coronado National Forest. While pets are generally welcome (if leashed), not surprisingly they're prohibited from the beach area.

There are two routes to Patagonia Lake. You could go south down I-19 as if you're headed to Nogales, then just before the border take Highway 82 and backtrack north about nineteen miles. Or consider the more scenic, and possibly faster, route down Highway 10 East to Highway 83. Turn south, and continue until the road takes you through Patagonia. There's no indication, but the park is seven miles further on, south of the town. A sign clearly indicates the turn, once you get that far.

From the turn, it's another 3.5 miles to the ranger station. There's a charge, which varies depending if you're there for overnight camping or just to spend the day. There's camping facilities with hookups, as well, so trailer and motor home owners are all set.

Patagonia Lake is only part of the sixty-acre Patagonia Lake State Park. It's the largest recreational lake in southern Arizona. Here you can fish, water ski, boat, swim, and hike. Since it's at 4,000 feet of elevation, it's generally a little cooler than Tucson at night, but the days are about the same in summer.

Water-skiing is allowed at the east end of the lake. If you're a fishing enthusiast, head to the west end. Fishing licenses are sold at the marina store, as are gear and supplies for both fishing and camping. You can rent or bring a boat, but do pay attention to the no-wake signs.

The ranger at Patagonia Lake State Park said this site has one of the highest visitor counts of the entire state. If you want a camping site, he recommended coming early Thursday night for a weekend stay. While there's some a.m. turnover, there are more than enough contenders for each site that opens up.

You can rent several different types of boats (paddle, canoe, or rowboat), or bring your own. The launching area is ample. There's also a small concession-operated store, so if you forgot the salt (or the sun block), you're not totally out of luck.

The mesquite trees scattered around the picnic and campgrounds provide welcome if dappled shade. More dependable are the ramadas, and each camp/picnic site has both a ramada and a grill. Drinking water, restrooms, and showers are all available.

Who says the desert is flat and uninteresting? As you return to Tucson from Patagonia Lake, elevation decreases. The road rolls, dips, and curves around mountains and through valleys. Notice when the vegetation changes. Near Patagonia Lake agaves and yuccas predominate. As you travel further north, more prickly pear and cholla are seen. Notice how the mesquite cluster along old waterways; remember, less than 100 years ago water was free-flowing through the Santa Cruz riverbed.

Finally the first saguaro appear, announcing your return to the Sonoran Desert. Then suddenly when you reach I-10 the valley opens up, and it's flat all the way to the Tucson and Catalina mountains.

If you travel this route in May/June/July, notice the differences between the blooms of some very similar cacti. Their colors range from white to yellow to red. Designed to attract flying pollinators, ground-level viewers may not be able to see the blossoms clearly. Visible to all are the bright red blossoms tipping the whip-like branches of the ocotillo, a favorite of local hummingbirds.

While there are numerous varieties of yucca, agave, and century plants, the plants within each group share basic similarities, and this is illustrated in the characteristics of their blooms. The century plant blooms on an erect stalk that branches high above the ground, each bloom cluster on a separate branch. Yuccas also bloom on sky-reaching stalks, but these blooms cluster together along the upper half, sort of like an elongated feather duster. Agaves strike a balance between the two, with loosely clustered blooms on multiple stalks.

The globular, ethereal-appearing yucca blooms may tempt you to bring the outdoors in, but resist. Several different types of insects escape the desert heat inside the blooms during the day. When the temperature cools down, the blossoms open and the nocturnal insects are freed. If the blossom stalk is inside your house, you have visitors!

Bisbee

Two other popular day trips that start from Tucson take you east on I-10 to Route 80 on into Bisbee and Tombstone.

Bisbee is about an hour's drive east of Tucson, and back into time about 100 years. Copper was discovered there in 1875 by a miner looking for gold or silver. Another miner, known for his stupidity, gambled away his claim by betting he could outrace on foot another man on horseback. Neither knew the value of what they had found. The one man who did know the value of what he'd found, Judge DeWitt Bisbee, wound up with the town named after him. He financed the Copper Queen Mine.

The town of Bisbee was once Arizona's largest and most prosperous city, with a top population of 20,000. It was a mining town with Victorian homes and a well-planned community. Today many of those homes have been converted into bed and breakfast inns, restaurants, and hotels.

The prosperity of the town rose and fell on the price and the demand for copper. There were many management versus union confrontations. One, the "Bisbee Deportation," made major headlines in 1917 and caused a national "outrage." The union efforts were defeated when armed sheriffs and deputies loaded 1,286 striking miners into boxcars and shipped them out, offloading them in the middle of the desert near Columbus, New Mexico.

You can tour the Queen Mine and the Lavender Pit (named after an executive of Phelps-Dodge Company, not the color of the ore) for a miner's-eye view. The latter is an open pit copper mine, over 950 feet deep and a mile long. There are also a number of museums, shops, and other points of interest to visit.

Tombstone

Tombstone is about another hour's drive south of Bisbee. This is the town made legendary by the Earp Brothers, Doc Holiday, and the gunfight at the OK Corral. Today it is basically a tourist town where you can see re-enactments of gunfights and what life was like way back then.

Aside from the gunfights, the heart of the town came from mining. More precisely, from giving the miners a good enough time that they didn't notice how much of their claim they left behind after a visit to town. The citizens who made a home there with families mined as much from the prospectors and partiers as they could.

The founder of the town, Ed Schieffelin, had been told that he'd sooner find his tombstone—what with all the Indians about—than gold or silver. They were dead wrong— he did find silver, and he named his claim "Tombstone" out of sheer cussedness.

By 1881 there were 5,000 people living there. The town was well known for its gambling, dance halls, brothels, and saloons. The town had 110 liquor licenses in 1882. (This must have been par for desert cities of those times. Doesn't this description sound pretty much like Tucson at the time?)

Of course, the situation couldn't remain that way for long—only seven years. Once the silver and gold gave out (estimated to have been some $40 million worth), there wasn't much to keep people there. Some stayed anyway. They figured if they could face seven years of the kind of treatment they'd already put up with, they could withstand the desert. Tombstone became "The Town Too Tough To Die." Take some time to see why.

Biosphere 2

Biosphere 2, another destination spoke from the hub of Tucson, lies in the opposite direction, about an hour north of Tucson on Oracle Road. Follow Oracle (it turns into Highway 77) through Oro Valley. When Highway 79 branches off to the left, you're about six miles from the turn to Biosphere 2. Turn at the sign and follow the road. Early on you pass under a large wooden arch announcing Little Hill Mining, Inc. Continue straight on to the entrance to Biosphere 2. It's not until then that you can catch a glimpse of the three-acre ecological system.

(For a while Oracle Road runs parallel to the west face of the Catalinas. Those who are more used to the southern aspect may be startled at the depth the range displays when seen from this angle. Here the elevation is higher than in the Tucson valley. Notice how the saguaro disappear just north of Rancho Vistoso, to be replaced by yucca. There's lots of mesquite and desert broom, and cholla are also abundant, but while prickly pears are seen, they're definitely in the minority here.)

Biosphere 2 began as a dream in the 1980s. The concept of Bioshphere 2 is to simulate an enclosed environment, similar to what space travelers might meet up with somewhere in the future. If another earth (Bioshpere 1) were needed, what would be required to make it? In 1991 the "Biospherians" were sealed inside it and lived there for seven months. The experiement was recently taken over by a consortium of scientists and educators. Today scientists and researchers go in and out the airlock on a regular basis. No more long-term stays are planned.

Visitors are welcomed on the site, for a fee. For $12.50 per person you can tour the public areas, either on your own or with a guided group, and walk through Biofair, science activities/exhibits housed under a large white tent-like structure.

The tour is a guided walk around the Biosphere 2 grounds. Both the walk and most of the time is spent viewing the outside (and peeking into the inside) of Biosphere 2. The three-acre totally sealed strucure contains living quarters, a rain forest, a savanah, a marsh, and an ocean, complete with waves and fish. Wear a hat, carry water, put on sunscreen. The tour/walk takes about an hour. It ends in an underground tunnel, viewing Biosphere's ocean from beneath the surface.

Drinking fountains and restrooms are scattered along the public routes. There's a small gift shop not far from the entrance that also sells snacks and drinks. A restaurant on the property, the Canyon Café, offers breakfast, lunch, and dinner selections. Last but not least, you can even choose to stay overnight at the Inn at the Biosphere.

Sports

The University of Arizona

If you live in Tucson and are a sports fan, you root for the Wildcats of the University of Arizona. You can fight the urge for a while, but sooner or later you're a Wildcat. There are a number of reasons for this.

First of all, The U of A has excellent sports teams.

The Wildcats football team's Desert Swarm defense made the cover of *Sports Illustrated* in 1995, and the team is usually a ranking contender, not only in the PAC-10 but nationally as well. Under the coaching of Dick Tomey the Wildcats have consistently won or seriously challenged the leading slot in the PAC-10 Conference and have consistently been rated among the Top Ten or the top twenty-five college teams in the United States.

The Wildcats basketballers are also championship contenders. Lute Olsen is their coach. PAC-10 champions or close to it, nationwide reputation, national rankings, and playoffs in the Sweet Sixteen and Great Eight, and working on achieving more, are typical accomplishments. Names like Steve Kerr, Sean Elliott, Kahlid Reeves, and Damon Stoudamire, recent U of A graduates, are readily recognized in the NBA.

The Wildcat Baseball Team, the Batcats, haven't done too well the last couple of years since they won the championship in 1993.

The Wildcats ice hockey team, the Icecats—yes, a hockey team in the desert—consistently score in the finals.

Another reason you'll become a Wildcats fan is because the professional teams that have such a presence on televised sports are sharing time with our college teams. We may not have a professional sports team (although the Phoenix Suns and Arizona Cardinals have been pretty much adopted), but our U of A teams, no matter what the sport, have achieved national recognition. You can just as easily find a Wildcat team on television on Saturday or Sunday as you would professional teams.

We don't mean to leave any of our U of A sports teams unrecognized. As a major university, our athletes—men and women—are recognized in track and field, cross country, golf, gymnastics, softball, soccer, swimming and diving, tennis, and volleyball. This excellence in sports is just another indication of the University of Arizona's contribution to Tucson.

The Copper Bowl

It seems that each year-end there are more college bowl games. The television coverage of bowl games and the public's desire to see them would bring them out of the woodwork if they couldn't happen any other way. One of those is the Copper Bowl. From Tucson's viewpoint it fits right in with the many visitors that find their way to us through the desert.

High School Sports

There is also an avid following of high school teams in all the sports. News shows on Friday nights announce high school scores. In a city the size of Chicago, for instance, that might take all night. But in Tucson, the teams are fewer and the interest greater.

One of the reasons for this popularity is that Tucson is the center for many of the outlying high schools from neighboring counties. There's a lot more than just local rivalry going on here.

Golf

You would think that Tucson's reputation as a resort and tourist town would provide a golf course or two. It does. In fact, there are ten public courses, eight semiprivate, six private, and four resort courses. (Not bad when you can measure the size of our city in terms of driving across town in about a half an hour.) No matter where you are in Tucson, if you get up early enough, you'll always find a game of golf available. Of course you may have to get in line for the best tee times.

Tucson's courses are not small-town. They have been designed by Robert Trent Jones Sr., Nicklaus, Stadler, and Fazio. In recent years the Tucson National Golf has been a PGA Tour Event. The Northern Telecom PGA Open plays at Starr Pass. The Randolph Municipal North Course hosts the Ping/Welch LPGA Championship.

The *Arizona Golf Guide* provides course reviews, quick reference guides, and an extended listing of clubs in Tucson and in other areas of Southern Arizona. It is published annually by *Tucson Guide Quarterly* and can be found anywhere a golfer might want to look.

Baseball

Tucson's warm, early springs are a natural to invite baseball. The Colorado Rockies hold spring training at Tucson's Hi Corbett Field. This expansion club of a few years has a large base of fans who follow them to Tucson each spring. The Tucson Toros, AAA Club for the Houston Astros, represent Tucson in the Pacific Coast League and also make their home at Hi Corbett Field. The Toros provide baseball fun and excitement for their many fans.

There is serious talk about expansion teams in baseball. Discussions about two new stadiums being built are underway. A new stadium has been approved for spring training for another major league club, and the White Sox are also considering holding their spring training here.

Tennis

The CIGNA Celebrity Tennis Classic is held in Tucson. This is the largest charity tournament in America and has raised more than $700,000 since 1982. For those who would rather play than watch, public courts are located throughout the city.

Biking

Thousand of cyclists and supporters and fans flock to Tucson each November for a bicycle race. Intergroup's El Tour de Tucson is held here and is the largest perimeter race in the country.

Soccer

As soccer becomes more and more popular in the United States, there will be more professional soccer teams. There are any number of soccer leagues in Tucson, and the teams are getting better. The Tucson Amigos represent the United States Interregional Soccer League. Those of us who grew up playing football or baseball might someday find ourselves outnumbered by the young men who play soccer.

Racing

If horse racing is your game, Tucson's Rillito Downs, just north of the Rillito River on 1st Avenue, races quarterhorses from November through spring. Greyhound Park offers year-round greyhound races, and yes, you can bet.

Tucson Raceway Park is the representative on the NASCAR circuit. (Check out their home page on the Internet. See Weblinks, page 220.) A dragstrip is in the planning stage.

Sports and Weather

The desert climate is very conducive to participative sports—except in the summer. You won't find many people on the tennis courts or golf course at 2:00 in the afternoon during the middle of the summer. (Well, golfers maybe. They've been known to put up with all kinds of hazards.) Tennis enthusiasts make it out there at 5:30 in the morning when it's already light and still comfortable enough to play. However, during the rest of the year you can play to your heart's content at any time of the day.

Hiking is always an alternative. The mountains and trails offer too many choices to list. You can also take walking tours of the city and our historic areas.

During winter, not only is it very comfortable to play practically any outdoor sport, winter sports are a short drive up the mountain. Mt. Lemmon offers skiing and snow to enthusiast.

CHAPTER FIVE

Modern Tucson

A city is a lot of things. When you get past all the definitions and descriptions, a city is primarily a location where many people live who have found a place where they can earn a living and support themselves and their families in relative safety and comfort. In the modern world of today, cities are economic centers.

Today, Tucson is, among all those other things we've uncovered, an economic center. Some cities were "economic centers" for many more years before Arizona became a state and Tucson became a modern city.

We live in a modern world where distance is no longer the factor it used to be. Mobility is taken for granted. People who work for IBM (I've Been Moved) know that Tucson is just another city on the list of possible relocations. Hughes Missile System employees can live just as easily in Tucson as they did in Southern California.

Tucson has experienced the same general economic impacts that the rest of the nation felt during World War I, the Depression, World War II, the postwar boom, and the recessions and recoveries of the 1980s and '90s. Some cities have fared better, some worse. Tucson still remains a strong economic center.

Like all other cities, technology has changed the nature of Tucson. It's no stranger to us: In 1917 Tucson had the first municipal airport in America.

Conditioning the Air

One of the technologies that had an important impact on Tucson was "air conditioning." The evaporative cooler (locally referred to as the "swamp cooler") was introduced in 1934. For many years it was called the "Arizona Cooler" because it so drastically changed the lives of people who lived in Arizona, and consequently Tucson.

The ability to cool air has had a significant impact on Tucson's economy. Because of the hot summers, businesses expected to have lower profits (if any) during those months. Most people who had the wherewithal simply left for cooler climes for the duration. It's hard to run profitable businesses when your customers are gone for three months of the year. When the lowly swamp cooler showed that cool air could be provided on a large basis, the air conditioning industry was born and Tucson had a means to survive the summer in our modern times.

Aside from all the jokes about "dry heat," Tucsonans rely on air conditioning to make life bearable during summer when they generally go from air-conditioned homes to air-conditioned cars to air-conditioned offices and stores.

Water

Living in the desert makes water one of Tucson's prime concerns. To continue to live in the desert makes conserving water and obtaining water one of the *sine qua non*s of the economy.

At one time Tucsonans relied on the Santa Cruz River to provide water and replenish the springs and washes in the area. Getting water 200 years ago was usually a simple matter of digging a hole or walking to the river. The town relied mainly on surface water. Even during the summer, water flowed in the Santa Cruz River and canals diverted it to crops and homes. The current century has drastically affected the river. It simply no longer flows, except as a result of major flooding during the winter rainy season or because of thunderstorms in the summer.

In the 1800s and early 1900s frequent floods eroded the riverbanks and changed the flood plain. The Tohono O'odham agricultural land south of Tucson was particularly affected.

In the 1930s, when centrifugal pumps were introduced, Tucson got more of its water from underground. Turbine pumps increased the flow of water, and water tables continued to drop. The city's ground-water wells increased from 11 in 1900 to more than 200 in 1980. Water customers jumped from 625 to over 558,000.

The demand on the availability of water outstripped nature's ability to replenish it. In 1980 the Ground Water Management Act was passed by the state. In the year 2001 Tucson (and other cities) must be able to show that it has enough water to support projected growth for the next 100 years.

The Central Arizona Project (CAP) is an aqueduct that runs from Lake Havasu on the Colorado River to Tucson, some 335 miles away. Lake Havasu supplies water for cities like Los Angeles, Phoenix, and Tucson. It is north of Needles, California, just about where Arizona, California, and Nevada meet. The cost of supplying water (it cost $4.4. billion to construct CAP) isn't really a consideration in the desert. If you don't have water, you won't be around.

The aqueduct was full when Tucson Water Company started pumping CAP water to about half of the city in November 1992. There was, however, a not-so-slight problem. Tucson's water mains and plumbing reacted to the different chemical makeup of the new water. Corrosion escalated, and old plumbing broke as a result. Water mains broke, pipes burst, dishwashers and other appliances (including swamp coolers) failed. This resulted in ruined walls, floors, rugs, and carpeting for those affected. To add insult to injury, the water stained laundry, looked horrible, and, worst of all, tasted bad.

The water source was switched back to ground water after there were so many complaints that there was no other choice. (Remember the dead cat thrown by an irate crowd many years ago?) The mess was cleaned up, but the problem is still not solved. At the present time, it appears that there are several options that will alleviate the situation, although none solves the problems completely.

One thing for sure, now that Tucson has the water, some way will be found to use it. Tucson uses enough water in a year to cover 110,000 acres of land one foot deep. Other cities also need water and are interested in CAP water. For example, many cities in California have introduced water rationing to stretch the supply of their water. With other cities and states clamoring for water, Tucson is aware that its allocation of CAP water is not something that can be allowed to flow away. So far the best plan seems to involve using CAP water to recharge the aquifer that now feeds our wells.

Service Industries

The largest overall employers in Tucson are service related. That includes city, county, and state workers, schools, hospitals and care facilities, regional offices of nationwide or state-wide companies, real estate agencies, insurance companies, and similar institutions, food and clothing stores, and restaurants.

Tucson's warm fall and spring and mild winter attract snowbirds. Retirement villages are scattered through the valley. These "villages" provide fall, winter, and spring homes for many retirees. They often provide shopping, recreational, craft, educational, and even dating opportunities for their residents. In late April and early May (sometimes as early as March) these retirement communities begin to empty as their residents head back to places that have finally become free of the snow and cold that make those places undesirable.

The terms "snowbirds" and 'Zonie appear throughout the book. Don't ever think that these terms are derogatory. Snowbirds are Tucson's winter visitors, and welcome ones they are. Some folks maintain a residence in Tucson for only a couple of months out of the year, usually that portion of winter when "back home" is at its most ridiculous. Others live in Tucson year round except for a couple of months; for some reason they usually choose to vacate sometime during the summer.

'Zonies are those Tucsonans who are here through the summer. Not only here, but proud of it! Well, why not? When it's as hot as an Arizona summer, pride is about the only thing that doesn't make you sweat more.

The annual exodus of snowbirds when the weather turns hot does have an upside for year-round residents. The streets are less crowded, public facilities see less traffic—you can get the tee time of your choice! Life moves at an even (believe it or not) more relaxed pace than usual. In the fall when its favorite visitors return, things pick up and Tucson's tempo again moves to a faster beat.

Davis Monthan Air Force Base

What was once the city's municipal airport is now Davis Monthan Air Force Base. Tucson had the first municipal airport in the nation. Charles Lindbergh dedicated the original runway in 1927. It was named after two Tucson natives who were killed in airplane crashes in the early 1920s. (Not too propitious a beginning, was it.) Anyway, the city and the Air Force shared the runways until 1947 when Tucson International Airport was built.

Davis Monthan plays a major part in Tucson's economy. After the State of Arizona and the University of Arizona, it is the third largest employer in Tucson. In 1994 it supplied 8,340 jobs for Tucsonans. Citizens sighed a collective sigh of relief when it was passed over in the last round for base closing in 1995. It appears that DM (as Tucsonans call it) will be around for quite a while.

During the cold war, DM was the base for SAC bomber squadrons. It also served as the regional headquarters for the Titan II missile sites scattered around Tucson. There is only one left in the world today. You can see it at the Titan Missile Museum (see page 160.)

Davis Monthan is perhaps best known as the boneyard for military aircraft. Take a drive south on Kolb Road to Escalante and you'll see why. There are literally thousands of aircraft parked out in the desert sun, mothballed. Stored and parked there are B-29s, B-52s, and jet fighters as well as propeller driven planes of all vintages and designs, from all branches of the armed services. Row upon row of planes, parked wing to wing or tail to wing, are lined up perfectly, as if they used a plumb line to do it. The small amount of rainfall and low humidity make for good storage. The caliche (pronounced cal-ee-chee) in the ground, baked by the desert, provides a surface that doesn't need to be paved and can withstand the weight of the planes.

Industry

Manufacturing plays a major role in the economy. Manufacturing employment in metropolitan Tucson has more than doubled in the past ten years. This growth is due to the increase of high technology manufacturers such as Hughes Missile Company, AiResearch, Sargent Controls, and Burr Brown, locating and expanding in Pima County.

During World War II many new industries opened as Davis Monthan Air Force Base brought many soldiers to the area, many of whom stayed after the war.

In 1951 Hughes Aircraft Company decided to construct a new manufacturing plant to produce electronics equipment. Hughes had as many as 5,700 employees in 1957.

In 1993 Hughes Missile Systems Company consolidated its manufacturing operations in Tucson. This brought about 3,000 new citizens to Tucson. (Hughes now has 7,275 employees.) There were additional benefits besides many new employees moving to town. The project cost $70 million and was completed in thirteen months. Some say the project was the biggest construction project Tucson has ever had, and it was all completed in a little over a year. Much of that construction money stayed right in Tucson because Sundt Corporation, headquartered in Tucson, won the construction bid. As a result, housing and construction also experienced a building boom. Service industries to support the growing population also benefitted from the move.

Other large private employers in Tucson include Circle K Corporation, First Data Corporation, IBM, Burr-Brown Corporation, Microsoft Corporation, Hillhaven Corporations, American Airlines, US West, Walgreen Drug Company, Weiser Lock, Inc., Westin La Paloma Resort, Allied Signal Aerospace Equipment Systems, Southern Pacific Transportation Company, Canyon Ranch, and Artisoft Inc.

NAFTA

The North American Free Trade Agreement (NAFTA) in general has been beneficial, although there is some un-

certainty about its future. Despite warnings of "loud suck-
ing sounds" to emanate from Mexico taking jobs, that hasn't
happened. It's too soon to have specific information about
its effects, but preliminary statistics indicate that U.S. exports to Mexico grew by 18 percent (three times greater
than to other countries) since its inception. An estimated
100,000 export jobs were created. Arizona's exports to
Mexico grew by 25 percent.

Sales of some consumer goods in Mexico are down because of its economy, but Arizona's sales to Mexico of equipment, appliances, tools, software, and other items have not
dropped. A Mexican word has come to be recognized despite
its length: maquiladoras (production and assembly plants).
There is an emphasis in trade areas about supplying and
supporting those plants. The Chamberlain Company (which
manufactures garage door openers and car polishing systems) has been in Nogales, Arizona for seventeen years and
has recently increased its investment. In Tucson, a new
Wal-Mart distribution center to service Mexico was established. Wal-Mart has expanded rapidly into Mexico in the
last three years and plans to have sixty-eight Wal-Mart
Superstores and SAM's Club stores. The 162,000-square-
foot merchandise distribution center here will support
those stores. The center has sixty trailer loading docks and
employs approximately two hundred people.

The report on NAFTA is still out. Congress hasn't yet
decided on whether it should leave it be or take some kind
of retroaction on it. The devaluation of Mexico's peso has
required U.S. intervention to support it, and it continues to
be weak. Hopefully, for Tucson, the United States, and
Mexico, the treaty will be a success.

Mining

Mining has been an essential part of employment in Tucson from the first pick and shovel prospector to the modern copper mines that dot our area. Copper mining on a large scale began in the Tucson area in the early 1870s. The "Electrical Revolution" found that copper filled its needs as a means to deliver electricity to homes and industry. The telegraph and telephone industries added to the list of industries who needed copper to deliver their products.

During World War I copper prices doubled because of the further expansion required by the war effort. Copper mining has produced more wealth in Arizona than mining efforts from precious metals like gold and silver. For example, in 1950 Arizona produced $130 million of copper, $15 million of zinc, $4 million of gold, and $4 million of silver. Arizona counts for about two-thirds of the copper produced in the United States, and about one-eighth of the world's supply. Copper remains the largest product of Arizona mines.

Magma Copper Company, a major mining company, is headquartered in Tucson. It currently employs about 3,600 people and operates a copper mine in Safford, about an hour's drive from Tucson north of the Santa Catalina Mountains. Asarco, Inc., another major mining company also has offices in Tucson and employs about 2,500 people.

Agriculture

Cotton has been grown in the area for centuries. Indians grew it for their personal use. During World War I the United States relied on cotton to provide uniforms for the doughboys. Modern methods of irrigation today produce an abundance of the crop.

Other agricultural crops that have been and are a significant element of the area's economy are citrus and pecan groves. For example, Orangegrove and Tangerine roads on the northwest side were logically named for the acres of citrus groves they led through.

Pecans have been grown in the area for years. An old pecan orchard that once grew near Ft. Lowell Park has been incorporated into a townhouse development. The venerable trees provide an atmosphere of park-like shade for the residents, as well as an annual source of pecans. If you drive south of Tucson, you'll most likely notice the large pecan groves along I-19 on the way to Green Valley.

The University of Arizona

Although some of Tucson's citizens would have preferred to have the state insane asylum instead of the University of Arizona when they were first established, the university has become one of the strongest pillars of our economy. Not only is it the largest employer in Tucson (10,100 jobs in 1994), its well-earned reputation attracts students, researchers, and professors from all over the world.

Tucson's ability to recognize what it is and then make the most of it has grown with the university from its beginnings. One of the most important elements businesses consider when choosing a city for relocation is the presence of a university with excellent students and graduates. The greater the caliber of its graduates, the greater interest technological businesses have in our area. The University of Arizona stands out as a prime example of "excellence attracts excellence."

Today, the U of A, like other modern universities across the nation, has had to tighten its belt. There is current discussion concerning major changes like the closing of the journalism and physical education departments. Since 1990 the university has reduced the number of jobs from 12,005 to 10,100.

The university has gained worldwide recognition in a number of fields. Its work in the field of optics illustrates this. University of Arizona scientists were entrusted with the delicate matter of helping make the spectacles for correcting the vision of the Hubble Telescope. They are also involved in future projects for Hubble such as NICMOS (Near Infrared Camera and Multi-Object Spectrometer) to be installed during a shuttle mission in 1997. This long-term interest in astronomy has led that industry to concentrate in Tucson.

The mountains surrounding Tucson have always made for good night viewing. Three major United States observatories are located in the mountain ranges nearby. Kitt Peak is located in the mountains west of Tucson. It was selected as the site for the National Observatory in the late 1950s. It has a four-meter telescope, the third largest in the United States.

The newest telescope on Kitt Peak, dubbed "WIYN," is delivering extremely sharp pictures, far better than were originally expected. WIYN's main mirror was cast and polished under the University of Arizona stadium by the University of Arizona's Steward Observatory Mirror Lab. The procedures used here result in a nearly perfect imaging system, closer to perfection than any other telescope mirror in the world.

Kitt Peak Observatory is also part of the Very Long Baseline Array which basically uses individual telescopes from locations stretching from Hawaii to the Virgin Islands to make one very large telescope.

Mt. Hopkins, in the Santa Rita Mountains to the south, has a 4.5 meter multiple-mirror telescope, the second largest in the United States. Mt. Hopkins is also involved in IOTA, the project to help earth-bound telescopes overcome the blurring effect of the atmosphere.

The fact that the University of Arizona has a world-class optics department has made Tucson the "optics capital" according to several national groups and publications. The Optical Sciences Center at the University of Arizona is the magnet for the cluster of companies who have moved here or developed here because of it.

Other companies are coming to Tucson attracted by the U of A and the quality of life. During 1995 Tucson's business activity continued to remain robust after a very strong 1994. In 1994 population grew by 24,000 people, the third largest increase on record. Hughes Missile Systems, Intuit (Quicken), and a large number of telemarketing/teleservicing companies moved here. The year 1995 saw Microsoft Corporation open a regional service center. The new companies that have moved here and the existing companies that have expanded, created many new jobs, something that is always good news for a city and its citizens.

Government

Federal, state, and local governments employ more than 60,000 people. The University of Arizona remains the largest single employer with about 10,000 employees. Davis Monthan Air Force Base has over 7,000 military and civilian employees.

Tourism

Tourism accounted for over $2.3 billion to the Pima County economy in 1995 and is a major part of its economy. New hotels have been constructed, and there is talk about major new construction of more in the downtown area.

Population

Recent population figures show Tucson's growth in the past years.

	1980	1990	1994
Tucson	330,537	405,390	440,335
Pima County	531,443	666,880	728,425
Arizona	2,716,546	3,665,228	4,071,650

Wages

One aspect of Tucson's employment—its wage levels—needs to be discussed. Wage rates are low in Tucson and in Arizona in general. There doesn't seem to be any known reason for this, because the cost of living is not consistent with the wage level. Some years ago it was "jokingly" referred to as "the sunshine adjustment." Supposedly the lower wages were a trade-off for the quality of life. Newcomers to the city usually find they have to make an adjustment to their salary expectations.

Tucson ranks 235 out of 310 metropolitan areas when it comes to salary levels. They are about $3,500 per year less than the Phoenix area, about $3,700 less than Las Vegas, and about $2,000 less than Salt Lake City and Albuquerque. With the influx of new companies, new technology, and business clusters, this will hopefully correct itself.

Pima County

Tucson is the county seat of Pima County. Pima County is the second largest county in Arizona. It was created in 1864 and includes most of the land that was acquired in the Gadsen Purchase. It covers 9,188 square miles and ranges in elevation from 1,200 feet to the 9,185 foot elevation of Mt. Lemmon in the Santa Catalinas.

The San Xavier, Tohono O'odham, and Pascua Yaqui Indian Reservations are in Pima County and comprise about 40 percent of the land. The State of Arizona, U.S. Forest Services, the Bureau of Land Management, and other public lands account for another 45 percent.

We've been saying all along that Tucson is a modern city, and we hope we've uncovered for you some of the things that have contributed to Tucson being what it is today.

Tucson wasn't always a city. It has been a place where people lived for many centuries. Sometimes that place was nothing more than a shady spot beside a spring in the middle of a desert. Sometimes it was a place where people could grow food for their families. Sometimes it was a fort where people took refuge from their enemies. We hope it is a place you enjoy, whether you live here or are just visiting.

For More Information

If you want more information about Tucson, its attractions and environs, we have provided the following information. Because hours, rates, and available services offered by places mentioned in the book are subject to change, below are telephone numbers and addresses for your use. Remember that the area code for much of Arizona changed. Tucson's area code is now 520.

Important Numbers

Arizona Motor Vehicle Division. Title, driver's license, and registration: Check white pages for location nearest you. 629-9808

Arizona Historical Society, 949 East Second Street, 628-5774

Arizona State Museum, At the University of Arizona, 621-6302

Arizona-Sonora Desert Museum, 2021 North Kinney Road, Information: 883-2702

Catalina State Park, 11570 North Oracle Road, 628-5798

Emergency: 911

Employment Information: 886-2145

Metropolitan Tucson Convention and Visitors Bureau, 130 South Scott Avenue, 624-1817

Pima Community College, 220 East Speedway, Course information: 884-6720

Police Information: 791-4452

Road Information: 573-7623

Sabino Canyon, Visitors Center: 749-8700, Shuttle information: 749-2327

SunTrans Rider Information Guide: 792-9222

Temperature and Weather: 881-3333

Tohono Chul Park, 7366 North Paseo del Norte, Information: 575-8468

Tucson Convention and Visitor Bureau, 260 S. Church, 800-638-8350

Tucson Parks and Recreation. A quarterly listing of their classes and programs can be picked up at any public library or neighborhood center. 900 South Randolph Way, Information: 791-4873

Tucson Botanical Gardens, 2150 North Alvernon Way, 326-9686

Tucson Metropolitan Chamber of Commerce, 465 West St. Mary's Road, Information: 792-1212

Tucson Airport Authority. For information on which airlines serve Tucson International Airport: 573-8100.

Tucson-Pima Library, downtown branch at 101 North Stone Avenue, Infoline: 791-401

University of Arizona, Visitor Center: 621-5130

Hiking Groups

SAHC (Southern Arizona Hiking Club) 50-60 hikes are offered monthly classified by mileage, terrain, elevation, and pace. Annual dues: $15 individual, $20 family. For more information on joining or attending a hike as a guest, call 751-4513.

The Sierra Club: 620-6401

The Senior Trekkers Club: (for those over 50) 520/296-7795

Ramblers Hiking Club, University of Arizona (don't need to be a student), 323-6418

Tucson Arts Organizations

a.k.a. Theatre, 125 E. Congress, 623-7852
Arizona Opera, 3501 N. Mountain Ave., 293-4336
Arizona Theatre Company, 330 S. Scott Ave., 884-8210
Ballet Arizona, 882-5022
Borderlands Theatre, 882-8607
Centennial Hall, University of Arizona, 621-3341
DeMeester Outdoor Performance Center, Reid Park, 791-4079
Gaslight Theatre, 7010 E. Broadway, 886-9428
Invisible Theatre, 1400 N. 1st Ave., 882-9721
Southern Arizona Light Opera Co., TCC, 260 S. Church Ave., 323-7888
Tucson Museum of Art, 140 N. Main, 624-2333
Tucson Philharmonia Youth Orchestra, TCC, 260 S. Church Ave., 326-2793
Tucson Symphony Orchestra, TCC, 260 S. Church Ave., 882-8585
UA Theatre Arts Dept., Park/Speedway, 621-1162
Tucson Jazz Society, hotline: 743-3399

Galleries

4th Avenue Gallery, 328 N. 4th Ave., 882-5584
Alamo Gallery, 101 W. 6th St., 882-9490
Armory Gallery, 307 S. 6th Ave., 629-9642
Art Forms Gallery, 137 E. Congress, 628-7047
Bero Gallery, 41 S. 6th Ave., 792-0313
Berta Wright Gallery Shops, 260 E. Congress, 882-7043
Bodhitree Gallery, 33 S. 5th Ave., 882-5195
Central Arts Collective, 188 E. Broadway, 623-5883
Citizens Transfer Art Studios, 44 W. 6th St., 882-5960
Dinnerware Artists Cooperative Gallery, 135 E. Congress, 792-4503
Etherton Gallery, 135 S. Scott Ave., 624-7370
F.L. Wright Gallery, 316 E. Congress, 622-3350
Howling Rabbit, 500 N. 4th Ave., 624-5676

Huntington Trading Co. Inc., 111 E. Congress, 628-8578

Image Gallery at The Screening Room, 127 E. Congress, 622-2262

Jose Galvez Photography and Gallery, 743 N. 4th Ave., 624-6878

Kathryn Wilde Photography, 459 S. Convent, 628-7313

Montanos Art Studio/Gallery, 136 W. 17th St., 624-8995

Old Town Artisans, 186 N. Meyer Ave., 623-6042

On Line Gallery and Salon, 545 N. 4th Ave., 622-9033

Phantom Galleries, 47 E. Pennington, 624-9977

Phantom Galleries, 110 S. Church/La Placita Village, 624-9977

Piney Hollow Time Line Gallery, 427 N. 4th Ave., 623-4450

Pink Adobe Gallery, 137 E. Congress, 623-2828

Puzey Gallery, 47 S. 6th Ave., 884-4522

Raw Studio/Gallery, 43 S. 6th Ave., 882-6927

Rosequist Galleries, 1615 E. Fort Lowell Road., 327-5729

Studio 113, 113 E. Broadway, 623-5167

Tucson Arts Coalition/Shane House Gallery, 218 S.4th Ave., 623-2577

Tucson Arts Coalition/Toole Shed Gallery, 197 E. Toole Rd., 622-3735

Shopping Centers

Crossroads Festival Shopping Plaza, Grant and Swan

El Con Mall, Broadway/near Country Club, 327-8767

Foothills Mall, 7401 N. La Cholla/Ina Rd., 742-7191

Fourth Avenue area, between 9th Street and University Blvd.

La Plaza Shoppes, 6530 E. Tanque Verde

Park Mall, 5870 E. Broadway, 748-1222

Plaza Palomino, corner of Swan and Ft. Lowell Road

Sixth Street Merchants, 6th St. south of UA campus

St. Phillip's Plaza, corner of Campbell Road and River Road

The Plaza/Williams Centre, 5340 E. Broadway Blvd.

Tucson Mall, 4500 N. Oracle, 293-7330

Tucson Web Links

Tucson is a study in contrasts, a "sleepy little ol' cow town" that at the same time is a major player in the micro component and optics industries. It's also in the forefront of computer technology, which is reflected in a plethora of Internet home pages. The following is a list of what you can find surfing the Internet. What better way to enjoy Tucson until you get here?

Tucson, Arizona

. . . . http://tucson.com/tucson/

CityNet's contribution to Tucson's Internet presence. Categories include News, Dating, Parks & Rec, Community, Restaurants, Business Directory, Housing, Schools, Economy/Jobs, Government, Mover's Aid, the Tucson weather forecast from Kitt Peak, and links to other Tucson/Arizona resources.

101 Things to Do–Tucson & So. AZ

. . . . http://www.arizonaguide.com/101/tucson/

The on-line version of the 101 list found in the *Arizona Guide*. Places, ideas, descriptions, background, phone numbers—even a link or two.

Tucson, Arizona links

. . . http://econ179.bpa.arizona.edu/JimHomePageFolder/
FaveLinksFolder/Tucson.html

This page is a link from a local gent, replete with Tucson links, publications, politics, educational and civic institutions, the arts, business, and "other stuff."

The Tucson Link

. . . . http://tucsonlink.rtd.com/

An Information and Telecommunications Forum presented by The Community Information and Tele-communications Alliance. An interactive public and private forum supporting the development and de-ployment of Tucson's information and telecommuni-cations infrastructure.

Tucson AZ Home Page

. . . http://www.Opus1.COM/emol/tucson/tucindex.html

Quite a rich site. Links to hundreds of Tucson-re-lated pages presented by *Entertainment Magazine On-Line* (EMOL). Included is: What To Do in Tucson (Events, Organizations, Arts Groups & Exhibits, and a *NightLife Guide*), Shopping & Dining in Tucson (Tucson Directory, Business Listings & Links, Com-mercial Home Pages, Downloadable Menus), Places To Visit in Tucson (Tucson Sites, Tourist Attrac-tions, Photo Tours), and More of Tucson (Media, Weather, Tucson Teen, Sports and Outdoors). There are also links to several Tucson businesses, as well as Tucson-related links not connected to EMOL.

Desert View High School Home Page

. . . http://wacky.ccit.arizona.edu/~susd/dvhome.html

Desert View is one of two secondary schools in the Sunnyside Unified School District in Tucson, Arizona.

The site was established in February 1995 with the help of the U of A. It includes some of the student's personal pages, an Educational LINKs Page with thousands of LINKs to "the interesting, the cool, and the educational." They also have a Native American Students Page under development.

The Tangle Web Inn
. . . . http://www.ctucson.com/so/ctucaz.html

This is actually a link from The Tangle Web Inn's Home Page, and has a number of neat links about and around Tucson, from the Tucson AZ Internet Yellow Pages to the Arizona Supreme Court. It's provided by Craycroft Hobbies, a hobby supply store in Tucson.

City.Net (Tucson, Arizona, United States)
. . . http://www.city.net/countries/united_states/arizona/tucson/

Links to Area Attractions, Business, City Guides, News and Weather, Parks and Outdoors, Sports, and Travel and Tourism (among others).

Tucson's Old Pueblo Trolley
. . . http://www.azstarnet.com/~bnoon/opthome.html

The Old Pueblo Trolley is an all volunteer, nonprofit organization that restores historic trolleys. Find out where to catch the trolley and what the schedule is. There are pictures of several of the trollies and (for those who are interested) links to other trolley-related sites.

El Adobe Restaurant
. . . . http://emol.org/emol/dining/eladobe.html

Curious about what you'll find at a Mexican restaurant? Check out El Adobe's page for a complete (downloadable) menu, including options and prices.

KVOA (Tucson's NBC Affiliate)

. . . . http://www.kvoa.com/

Your source for news, weather, sports, and local program notes, as well as links to NBC and NBC shows.

Tucson Tee Time

. . . . http://www.emerald.net/golf/

A comprehensive listing of all the municipal, private, public and resort golf courses in Tucson, Arizona and the surrounding areas. A basic description is given of each course including address, course professional, phone number, holes, par, yardage, facilities, and rates. A nice resource for the golfer.

Tucson Raceway Park, Tucson, AZ

. . . . http://www.primenet.com/~thomasj/trp.htm

Check the Raceway's NASCAR schedule for the year or the NASCAR point standings.

Sabino Canyon National Recreation Area

. . . http://dizzy.library.arizona.edu/images/sabino/ homepage.html

A celebration of this natural delight, this is an electronic walk through Sabino Canyon, including photos and links to other sources of information about the canyon.

Reid Park Zoo

. . . http://www.tucson.com/outback/public_service/ reidpark/

This page is provided by a member of the Tucson Zoological Society and is maintained for information only. It is not sanctioned by either the Reid Park Zoo, Tucson Zoological Society, or Tucson Parks & Recreation Department. It is, however, a great way to get information about Reid Park Zoo: What's New at the

Zoo!, Upcoming Events, and links to the Tucson Zoological Society, the Arizona-Sonora Desert Museum, the Phoenix Zoo, ZooNet, and ZooLinks.

Kitt Peak - Public Page
. . . . http://www.noao.edu/pubpage/pub.html

Wonder what Kitt Peak National Observatory has to offer? Check out this page for Travel Information (including a map), What's On Kitt Peak?, and Visitor Information (with hours and telephone numbers).

Coronado National Forest
. . . . http://www.gorp.com/gorp/resource/ us_national_forest/az_coron.htm

This site is maintained by the U.S. National Forest Service. First there's a short history of the Coronado forest, then a listing of points of interest (some with links of their own), recreation opportunities, and District Ranger Stations (including addresses and telephone numbers).

Saguaro National Park
. . . . http://www.gorp.com/gorp/resource/ US_NATIONAL_PARK/az_sagua.htm

Everything you ever wanted to know about the saguaro, the mightiest of cacti, is here for you. There's also information on how to make your visit to either Saguaro National Park East or West a pleasant experience.

Ramsey Canyon Preserve
. . . . http://hanksville.phast.umass.edu/defs/ independent/AZNC/Ramsey.ht ml

This 300-acre preserve, located 87 miles southeast of Tucson, 10 miles south of Sierra Vista, is one of those maintained by the Nature Conservancy. It's most remarkable for the 14 species of hummingbirds that have been seen at the canyon between April and October.

University of Arizona

. . . . http://www.arizona.edu/

The Home Page of the University of Arizona. Check out current announcements, or look up Student Information, Academics, Research, University Business Services and Administration, the University outside the campus, Places to Go, Things to Do, Publications, News and Information, and more.

Arizona Daily Wildcat

. . . . http://info-center.ccit.arizona.edu/~wildcat/

The newspaper of the University of Arizona. News, sports, comics, letters, Mutato, and a searchable morgue—who could ask for anything more?

The University of Arizona Library

. . . . http://dizzy.library.arizona.edu/

Everything you could possibly want to know about the UA Library, its resources, other Internet resources, links to other UA sites, and search engines.

HomePage for UA Sports

. . . . http://komodo.hacks.arizona.edu:80/sports/

A private page dedicated to the Wildcats, all the Wildcats! Includes indices of Sports and Club Teams, Players, Coaches, and Schedules for the UofA Teams, with various sports links.

Pima Community College

. . . . http://www.pima.edu/pcc_www.html

This site provides links to information resources, the various campuses of Pima College, as well as Pima Community College Departmental Home Pages

(Academic Advising, Athletics, etc.) and Personal Home Pages at PCC.

PCC Tucson Info

. . . . http://www.library.pima.edu/tucson.html

A compilation of Tucson-related links maintained by the Pima Community College Library.

KUAT Online

. . . . http://info-center.ccit.arizona.edu/~kuat/kuat1.html

The World Wide Web Home Page for the KUAT Communications Group, an educational broadcast and production resource of the University of Arizona consisting of KUAT-TV (Channel 6 locally), Classical KUAT-FM, KUAT-AM/KUAZ-FM, and VideoServices. Program guides, news, press releases, and other information about the KUAT Communications Group.

The Arizona Guide

. . . . http://www.arizonaguide.com

Arizona's official site, maintained by the Arizona Office of Tourism. A definite bookmark! Here are links to information about Arizona's cities, weather, golf, and the Grand Canyon, with downloadable maps and information on accommodations, as well as a calendar of events. Explore Arizona by Territory: Canyon Country, Indian Country, High Country, Central Country, Golden Country, River Country, and Old West Country, each with short descriptions of local attractions and sources for more information.

The Arizona Star

. . . . http://www.azstarnet.com

The electronic version of *The Arizona Star*. This on-line newspaper contains the daily edition of the

Star. It also provides internet access for StarNet subscribers.

The AZConnect Community
. . . . http://www.getnet.com:80/azconnect/

AZConnect is an exclusive political and public affairs system on the Internet. AZConnect, which originates from Phoenix, Arizona (USA), is one of the first statewide systems designed for constituents of the digital democracy band.

Arizona World-Wide Web Servers
. . . . http://www.eas.asu.edu/az/servers.html

Just what it says: a list (some with a short description) of WWWeb servers in Arizona, provided by the Arizona State University College of Engineering and Applied Sciences.

Arizona Destinations
. . . . http://www.amdest.com/

This site opens with a link to the Arizona Internet Yellow Pages, then breaks subsequent information into categories: Arizona Cities, Arizona Attractions, Arizona Lodging, Arizona Services, Arizona Dining, Online Shopping, Arizona Golf Central, Arizona Sports, Arizona Kids Net, Arizona Photographer's Gallery, and don't forget the always popular Pat Paulsen for President!

Grand Canyon National Park Home Page
. . . . http://kbt.com/gc/gc_home.html

NOT to be missed. The "unofficial" Grand Canyon National Park Home Page. Obviously maintained as a labor of love, after perusing the links on this page the obvious next step is a visit in person. If that isn't a possibility, however, check the gallery for spectacular photographs of this glorious creation of nature, including wildlife and flora.

American Indian Resources
. . . . http://www.ihs.gov/Paths/AI.html

This is a link from the Home Page of the Indian Health Service. Dozens of Native American links, from information (general or specific) to scholarships to recipes.

American Indian Resources II
. . . . http://hanksville.phast.umass.edu/misc/NAresources.html

Self-billed as the "Index of Native American Resources on the Internet," this is a rich resource for anyone looking for information on anything Native American-related.

Southwest Jewish Archives
. . . . http://dizzy.library.arizona.edu/images/swja/swjalist.html

A site dedicated to the contributions of Jewish pioneers in the United States Southwest. Contains many interesting links to related subjects.

Picacho Peak State Park
. . . . http://159.87.28.204/parkhtml/picacho.html

John and Donna Kamper (e-mail address)
. . . . jdk@azstarnet.com

Index